50 YEARS

SAGE was founded in 1965 by Sara Miller McCune to support the dissemination of usable knowledge by publishing innovative and high-quality research and teaching content. Today, we publish more than 750 journals, including those of more than 300 learned societies, more than 800 new books per year, and a growing range of library products including archives, data, case studies, reports, conference highlights, and video. SAGE remains majority-owned by our founder, and on her passing will become owned by a charitable trust that secures our continued independence.

Los Angeles | London | Washington DC | New Delhi | Singapore

Advance Praise for
Work Sucks! Or Do You?

'In a world where we are known merely by how successful we are, Anshul Chaturvedi's book is a refreshing wake-up call. Because life is not as easy as it seems to be, nor is success the only barometer of achievement at the workplace. Anshul drives home many practical points in an inimitably lucid in-your-face style, thus getting rid of the cobwebs of both niceties and waffling. It is a compelling read for those not just planning to enter their working lives, but equally for those entrenched at work: many of whom feel a certain heartbreak at their own seeming inadequacies. He deftly weaves patterns across sectors and uses poignant examples from Bollywood to Vivekananda, to drive home points mired in reality.'

—Suhel Seth, author of *Get to the Top: The Ten Rules for Social Success*

'This immensely readable leadership book has a misleading title. The author, Anshul Chaturvedi, never takes this distillation of workplace wisdom or himself too seriously in this book. This is both his strength as well as his weakness. He presents a timeless philosophy of work, as irreverently as a cafe conversation. Sample this marvellous insight from the book: Solidarity in the office gang means the gang buddies not telling you that it was your mistake, ever. It also, therefore, means you never correct your mistakes till it's too late to do anything about them anymore.

This book would go straight to the heart of the run-of-the-mill MBAs, who often mistake expertise as excellence. While expertise is about possessing a bundle of skills, excellence comes from dispossessing the ego that enhances one's capacity to effectively apply those skills in the job. The author says, for instance, once you have fulfilled the need for which you were hired, you always, always have to cater to a higher need or risk, being irrelevant.

Drawing on perennial principles of workplace leadership, the author makes ancient wisdom very accessible to first-time managers as well as veterans in the job. The tone is intimate and enriched with the author's first-hand experiences of professional life. The many anecdotes of the book hang like many coloured beads on the thread of an enduring philosophy of work. Some insights dazzle like a rare gem. This is a refreshingly resplendent work. If I have felt the urge to read every page in a management book in a long time, this has to be one such book. I would unhesitatingly recommend this to anyone who wants to figure out what a philosopher worker or *karmayogi* is all about.'

—**Debashis Chatterjee**, author of *Timeless Leadership* and director, IIM Kozhikode

'The philosophical and transcendental find a connect with something as severe as a competitive career in a global economy. Anshul shares his unique take on navigating the daily *kurukshetra*s. Anshul has bone-deep honesty in his writing [and is] absolutely unapologetic about his approach; he honestly shares the minutest of his observations and weaves in life philosophy.'

—**Prasoon Joshi**, lyricist, screenwriter, advertising guru and copywriter

'Technology, convenience, upward mobility, economic and cultural reforms are all on the rise, yet problems abound both professionally and personally that are simultaneously timeless and avant-garde in nature. Chaturvedi calmly dismantles entitlement, drama (and often trauma) at the workplace to provide a nuts and bolt analysis on *how* to work eschewing the what, where, when and with who that corporate czars and teeny boppers alike are inordinately concerned with. In my psychology work around the world, one of the biggest issues is not having a philosophy or compass for guidance when the proverbial stuff hits the fan. *Work Sucks! Or Do You?* is a pithy philosophical manual that will force one to get it together, benefiting both the individual and collective.'

—**Anjhula Mya Singh Bais**, PhD, model and actress

'Few books have impressed me as much as this one in its uniqueness, creativity, impact, effectiveness and frankness—this lucid, open hearted, fascinating account makes interesting and informative reading for young people wanting to make a success out of their career. It is an insightful and thought-provoking read.'

—**Amitabh Kant**, author of *Branding India: An Incredible Story*

WORK SUCKS!
OR DO YOU?

THE TASK OF ZORRO!

WORK SUCKS!
OR DO YOU?

ANSHUL CHATURVEDI

www.sagepublications.com

Los Angeles • London • New Delhi • Singapore • Washington DC

First published in 2015 by

SAGE Response
B1/I-1 Mohan Cooperative Industrial Area
Mathura Road, New Delhi 110 044, India

SAGE Publications Inc
2455 Teller Road
Thousand Oaks, California 91320, USA

SAGE Publications Ltd
1 Oliver's Yard, 55 City Road
London EC1Y 1SP, United Kingdom

SAGE Publications Asia-Pacific Pte Ltd
3 Church Street
#10-04 Samsung Hub
Singapore 049483

Published by Vivek Mehra for SAGE Publications India Pvt Ltd, Phototypeset in 11/14 pts ITC Century Book by RECTO Graphics, Delhi and printed at Sai Print-o-Pack, New Delhi.

Library of Congress Cataloging-in-Publication Data

Chaturvedi, Anshul.
  Work sucks! : or do you? / Anshul Chaturvedi.
    pages cm
  Includes bibliographical reference.
  1. Job satisfaction. 2. Employee motivation. 3. Career development.
I. Title.
  HF5549.5.J63C43   650.1—dc23   2015   2014043528

ISBN: 978-93-515-0069-8 (PB)

The SAGE Team: Sachin Sharma, Sanghamitra Patowary and Nand Kumar Jha
Cover illustration: Thinkstock.com

To all those young people—girls, mostly, actually—who, in the course of making and unmaking their careers in my vicinity over the past decade and suffering both their trauma and my lectures along the way, actually taught me most of this in a textbook case of reverse mentoring. Someday, I hope to repay the debt.

Thank you for choosing a SAGE product! If you have any comment, observation or feedback, I would like to personally hear from you. Please write to me at <u>contactceo@sagepub.in</u>

—Vivek Mehra, Managing Director and CEO,
SAGE Publications India Pvt Ltd, New Delhi

Bulk Sales

SAGE India offers special discounts for purchase of books in bulk. We also make available special imprints and excerpts from our books on demand.

For orders and enquiries, write to us at

Marketing Department
SAGE Publications India Pvt Ltd
B1/I-1, Mohan Cooperative Industrial Area
Mathura Road, Post Bag 7
New Delhi 110044, India
E-mail us at <u>marketing@sagepub.in</u>

Get to know more about SAGE, be invited to SAGE events, get on our mailing list. Write today to <u>marketing@sagepub.in</u>

This book is also available as an e-book.

Contents

Preface

The making of a non-self-help book

Midway through the drafting of this book, when I was passing around notes for feedback in the hope that at least someone would say something nice about it, a colleague read halfway through a chapter, paused as if to decide whether it was appropriate to ask the question, made up her mind and then asked me—'All this that you're trashing, these things that you say we mustn't do, but all that's *natural*, right? Of course people of our age react this way. What else would we do?'

That was a valid point. It's because I see so much of it as 'natural' that I wrote this book, as unless it's actually flagged as dangerous for you, stuff that you may pick up naturally—such as cigarettes as a solution for college stress—can make you pay in the long run. But the long run isn't something you think of too often when you're starting out at work, at your first or second job perhaps, in the initial years. It's boring. Life is not about all this analysis, over thinking, processing, is it? And you're never going to turn 30, never going to have to look back at your first decade at work, never look around at your professional peer group, never risk seeing your colleague become your boss five years down the line and wonder if what you did was the best that you could have, right?

But I meander. Let me make one thing clear: I don't really get what self-help books are about, and I'd really be embarrassed if this was to be seen as 'self-help'. Self-help *gyaan* is delivered by experts or by people who are very famous or very happy. I am none of the three. And I find too much of what is peddled as self-help overly cheesy and set in wonderland. I don't think a positive mindset will suffice to get you all that you wish for, no. I'm in my 40s now, and I've been waiting for the bloody universe to conspire to give me what I really want for about 20 years, and it's a very shoddy conspiracy so far. I am not a fan of the schools of positive thought whose advocates look like a still from a toothpaste ad all the time. Bring me the company of the unsmiling, low-expectation, coffee-addicted mavericks anytime.

This book was, therefore, not written for *self-help*. It was written as nothing more than an office equivalent of the warning board before an unmanned railway crossing. It will not make you the CEO of Microsoft or the youngest billionaire in Faridabad, the week after you read it. It will not give you quotable quotes to use in lectures. It will not explain to you how to run an airline or a steel plant.

But it'll try to tell you how *not* to run yourself. And until you have your *funda*s clear about that, the rest doesn't really matter; you could be gifted an airline on your 18th birthday and still have the damn fleet grounded before you're 24. Or be gifted a movie and make people weep while watching it for all the wrong reasons. Or be gifted a political party in power and have it grounded as well before you're 44.

This book came from questions about how we so often get the basics of working so very wrong in a way which doesn't seem wrong to us at all since, to go back to the beginning, it is all so *natural*.

My limited take on this is: From what I remember of Prince Siddhartha's trip with his charioteer, there is a lot which we can't help which is natural. Sickness is natural and unavoidable. Ageing is natural and unavoidable. Death is natural and unavoidable.

Spending the first five years at work in a haze of trauma, bitterness, tears, texting, ranting, occasional senseless giggling and an overall sense of having been dealt a raw deal by the boss, the company and the universe, all collaborators in a gigantic conspiracy against you is, however, neither natural nor unavoidable.

I wrote this book to suggest, in all humility, that there may be simpler ways to live your life and do your work as you set out to build a career. It is, in a sense, attempting to reduce the volume of the background music playing *naturally* around you, so you can perhaps hear a few things which don't always get your attention. This is not about the universe, self-help experts, keeping your job safe in the current economy, how to manage your boss, how to build better equations with colleagues, how to impress clients or any of that.

And I can't tell you all that, in any case. While sorting thoughts in my head long, long before they came together in the form of this book, what I was looking to do was to save some time and energy, perhaps some years, too, of people who could easily use the workplace as a tool to build themselves, but were, more often than not, fighting it instead and wearing themselves out. If having a job and going to office leaves you feeling that life sucks infinitely more now than it did before you started working, there's something going fundamentally—even if naturally—wrong. So, you need to have a clear idea of what is going wrong, and perhaps a vague idea of how to stop it.

That is about all that I am trying to communicate.

Those of you lucky enough to be upbeat and enthusiastic about going to work six days in a week and having fun while at it—you don't need to read this. Spend the money on a pizza instead. This is for the rest of us.

Introductory essay: Why is it so unfair?

The idea of this book came about from two things.

One, I find it difficult to be inspired by words like *managerial ethics* or *employee motivation*. I have a pressing personal need to have a *philosophical* anchor to have total clarity about why I do things and *how*, else I'm totally disinterested—and then I can't do them well enough. I found that anchor, quite by accident, not in a billionaire tycoon's managerial *gyaan*, but in the assorted ramblings of a monk who had very little money throughout life and died at 39. At 39, realising that I'd done nothing much with my life while he'd made his mark and departed by that stage, I attempted to crystallise what little I'd understood of life—or at least life at the workplace. So this has emerged over a two-year period, and therefore by the time it comes to you, tragically, I'm not in my 30s anymore. Perhaps, after spending money and having read it, you'll wish I'd died at 39 too and spared you the atrocity.

On the other hand, you may just see it as a reality check of some passing relevance, whether you're 19 or 39. Either way, it'll be interesting. SRK flamboyantly says that he doesn't work anymore for either prosperity or posterity. Writing books very rarely gets you prosperity, so at best one can hope that one has connected to that odd thought which will make someone think. And thoughts last. So, a sort of pseudo-posterity is what I guess all of us who haven't established ashrams or industries, but still have the audacity to write something remotely approaching a self-help book are aspiring for. I plead guilty, however, of aspiring for both prosperity and posterity.

The second thing was in the decade between 30 and 40, seeing so, so many younger people handle their own equivalents of my angst and cynicism and pressure in depressingly and amazingly repetitive, unproductive, angsty, self-destructive ways. I am angsty, too, but I try to keep a sense of detachment; thanks to what garbled comprehension of the Gita my mind could gather. On *so* many occasions, I have been bemused by the manner in which the young worker handles work pressures and challenges in the beginning of his/her career. And I totally get it when someone in Japan decides to create places where workers can go across in the lunch hour and smash plates against a wall. Ideally, against a wall which has a pic of the boss. That's what a lot of people want to do throughout the day in office.

Do offices really care about that? At a very basic level, I think not. Why do people burn themselves out in emotional drama, then, without really adding too much to their skills or their standing? In their own perspective, they are usually perfectly justified. To their bosom buddies, they are more than perfectly justified, and if the collective feelings of angsty buddies were to have had more visible ramifications, divine retribution would have struck down lots of offices with a combination of lightning and earthquakes. But divine retribution happens in its own time, and we don't even know if we will live long enough to see it. So we need to find our solutions, like, *now*.

When I have a captive audience, I often like to give the immune system parallel—the factors that lead to angst and bitterness and shrieking lunacy will float around us just as inevitably as viruses will. There's *nothing* you can do about the microbe-carrying air or other people and processes. Whether or not that leaves you sick every third day depends on *your* immune system. That's the *only* thing you can do anything about. Mommy told you to take vitamin C to avoid catching the cold, but didn't tell you how to build your immunity to everyday stress. If you haven't worked on your immunity, you're walking around with the equivalent of emotional AIDS. Your own weakness will finally rob you of energy, while you keep blaming the disease. Others can handle that disease because their immune systems are robust enough. You can't. Understanding that is the first step in restoring sanity or mental fitness.

The bulk of the early years of many young professionals see a massive amount of energy wasted in angst, friction and a fundamental lack of understanding of:

- how workplaces function, and
- how they can grow as individuals while working.

They tend to see the two things as, at best, separate, and at worst, opposites. I have first-hand often experienced that a young professional who is able to correlate some basics of his/her life to his workplace, and is able to see that he/she will find answers to what irks him/her first within *himself/herself*—and not in some specialised management theory manual—is infinitely more capable of dealing with the ups and downs of office in a detached, philosophical way (*philosophical* is not a word to be embarrassed about, OK, it's very 'yo'), and finally does better and more sustained work than either the nail-biters or the chronic intriguers.

My basic point, which you will find running as a primary undercurrent through the pages that follow, is about a very clear hierarchy in which *how* you work is a far more important thing for you to resolve than what you do at work. Far too many of us are obsessed with *what* we do and leave the question of fundamentally *how* we do it, if the question even crosses our mind, to our supervisory systems. The thought of treating the basics of *how* you work as the headache of whoever currently pays your salary is as unrealistic as leaving the basics of running your country's value system to MPs. The end result will be as ad hoc and messed up.

Vivekananda will occasionally keep popping up in all this, even though he was no MBA or marketing whiz. That's because the way I approach many of my basic life questions emerged from a Vivekananda-centric prism, and I found them so spot-on in resolving questions about work so often that I rarely needed to turn to what experts in management were saying. In any case, it's not as if I was (or am) running a billion-dollar conglomerate. Many of his answers worked and have sufficed for me. Some of them gave me a direction to go beyond and find my own answers. While Vivekananda may not have been a student or a teacher of management theory, and many young people may never have needed to refer to him in a *personal* searching-for-meaning capacity either, the fundamental truths that he taught are surprisingly applicable in today's workplace—a workplace where many of us are ambitious and impatient and often resentful of the way things run, of the relative (even if transitory) success of others and fray quickly when things don't go our way as soon as we have started working, and people refuse to promptly realise that we are God's chosen gift to the workplace.

To my mind, this book is a series of mental conversations with: (a) the young worker coming to terms with the emotional, social and psychological challenges that the initial years of work bring, and (b) the relatively older professional who is getting enveloped in self-defeating reflexes, is therefore not going to grow any further or better and doesn't realise it yet. The emotional and social fallouts of office functioning—praise, flak, gossip, roles, comparisons, angst, loyalties—take over almost all the mental space of the young professional, at least till such time he/she is—theoretically—able to find a mental and philosophical balance. In some cases, he/she never does. Smart self-marketing jargon and the Dale Carnegie brand of handling behaviour and responses are, to my mind, band-aid solutions. Workers who have faced the pressures and the unhappiness that the often fundamentally largely unemotional/non-compassionate workplace brings and have lost sight of the larger picture along the way as they fill themselves to the brim with *this place sucks* thoughts may find this as something to refer to when they don't know how to handle things *without themselves diminishing as people.* There is, after all, at least to my mind, little point in attaining a work goal in a manner that makes you a smaller person. Office will go at some point of time. When you're dying, you need to look at that mirror and cockily tell yourself you didn't sell your soul for edging ahead by that extra 5 per cent in the career rat race, don't you?

Many people in their 20s and 30s find an angsty *F*** IT* as the first response to a workplace problem they can't handle. Oh, it's your response too, is it? Sounds really, really cool when you say it to three friends gathered admiringly around you in the cafeteria or at the smoking joint behind the office. Tragically, though, there's only so much that you can *F*, you know? And the office, which as this large impersonal shapeless collective organism, is sometimes saying 'F YOU!' right back at you and doesn't give a damn for your angst beyond a point. Now, while you're in the *F all* mood and at the same point of time you realise your parents don't understand you at all and your boyfriend is turning out to be a total lout and your life is all out of gear, umm, maybe it's time to check if the angst overdose is centred around *your* approach to life? Do your mind a favour. If that's the way things look, take some time out to *think*—rather than rant—because if you stay on that mental track, chances are 10 years from now you'll be what your friends today call a certified loser. Maybe that should be Certified Loser.

This book's fundamental space is in a zone somewhere between the Effective Habits or the Don't Sweat The Small Stuff, on the one hand, and Sarvapalli Radhakrishnan's commentary on the Gita or the Letters of Swami Vivekananda, on the other—but with all its philosophy, focus and ready references condensed and focused on the workplace and you, to suggest that perhaps you don't have to stop growing as a person, emotionally and philosophically, as you go about earning your daily bread. This is not *religious*. This is essentially Give Me This Day My Daily Bread Without Me Having to Feel Like a Loser to Earn it.

Additionally, while I have often dipped into what the Gita or Vivekananda has taught me, I do not see this as an India-centric read. Vivekananda came to the West to teach spirituality from a land that had—at that point—no economic stature to speak of. The West, therefore, has never seen him as someone whose thoughts are applicable to the workplace. In a sense, I am attempting to repay the debts, in-absentia Eklavya style perhaps, to my original teacher by attempting to reintroduce Vivekananda as a thought processor for handling workplace angst and issues, not just as a monk in saffron. And there are interesting overlaps and common zones between the best of Western practical workplace thinkers and the most abstract philosophy of the Vedanta, which Vivekananda swore by. Finally, what's good for your life is good for your office. Half your life is spent there anyway. More than half, actually, if you count just the waking hours.

I also have often had long arguments with those who give up on trying to change themselves with a cynical, disdainful belief in 'it's all about connections/godfathers/chance/networking/gender/caste/whatever.' I keep arguing that to make the immediate senior the focus of this much angst and to attribute everyone's growth to personalised factors is oversimplifying things to a degree of stupidity. It is only the average player who has to keep the Board happy all the time. Sachin Tendulkar never *really* needed to worry who ran the BCCI, beyond a point, or even who the captain was. His brand equity made the hierarchy irrelevant. If he were to be dropped from a Test, the BCCI would be more stressed than he would. Salman Khan doesn't really need a director to position him—you often forget who directed his films. They're just *his* films. All of us can break the stranglehold of the supposed hierarchy if we are good enough. An employee who is worth five times the salary he gets isn't subject to the usual uncertainties about job security anymore. On the other hand, Bollywood is full of kids with dads bringing in cash in trucks and pouring it into marketing and publicity budgets. But the poor kids can't act, period. They flop and flop and flop. And are re-launched over and over again. What *can* a godfather do, beyond a point? If you don't have one, good for you. Perhaps you won't do too much in life. But if you *do*, at least it'll be 100 per cent *you*.

Those of us who want to do good work, who *enjoy* doing good work, who derive internal satisfaction from doing what we at least *think* is good work—we need to reconcile to the reality that, at least in the short run, *rewards* are very eccentric and unpredictable in nature. To expect work to be lauded instantly will land you with the same heartbreak that a Raj Kapoor or a Sanjay Leela Bhansali faces when *Mera Naam Joker* or *Khamoshi* crashes at the box office. CEOs who do great work end up being sacked, generals who fight brilliant wars end up being imprisoned, directors make astonishingly beautiful films only to find the crowds buying tickets to 'item number' movies instead, politicians who genuinely work for reform lose to those who work the caste equations better in the campaigning phase. This is how it so often is. Stop being surprised by it. It's not—'why does this happen to me, God?' It happens to *everybody*.

There is, of course, one key factor which negates a lot of things written and said, when you are hassled and confused or losing out on your career, on your mental stability in your younger years—time. A 45-year old handles a couple of tough years far more easily than a 25-year old does, and there's good reason for that. In your 20s or even later, sometimes all the *gyaan* is so irritating, since the back of your mind has this clock ticking away, saying *how long* do I put up with this? If someone else gets ahead by hook or by crook, if we don't get the breaks we so desperately wanted, if your cousin keeps posting FB pictures of the US vacation that his/her salary enables him/her to take while your salary account runs out of cash by the 24th of each month, there's that sense of having missed the bus.

It may look that way to you, fair enough. But that's not necessarily true.

But here's how I see it: You can start and zip off on a 100-cc bike in all of three seconds. At that point, the pilot of a 777 airliner or, for that matter, the captain sailing the Queen Elizabeth 2 can't race you. Sometimes, careers look like that. The plane will stand still and just rev and rev its engines, while the bike has already shot off a couple of miles into the horizon. The ship will idle away and take hours just to get engines to full speed. But *once* it starts, the plane will travel at a speed which the bike never can match up to. So if you're counting 0–15 minutes, the bike beats the plane in distance travelled. If you're counting 0–6 hours, though, we're not even going to compare. Sometimes, careers—and lives—that have to go a long way can take a long time to take off. When someone sympathises with me or with someone else, at not quite being the sprinty bike—for instance, when a student just out of an IIT or IIM or DU is placed in his first job on a salary which I still aspire for after 15 years of my limited career in journalism—I tell them, 'Hey, I'm revving, wait till I take off!' And no, I don't say it just for effect. I may not have a very high run rate, but I'm still at the halfway stage of my innings, so don't predict the final score just yet.

If you haven't got off to a blistering start in the first 10 overs of your innings, don't shoot yourself. Many a match has changed course even in the last 10. Give yourself time. Many apparently great careers don't lead anywhere. Many cars overtaking us at blindingly mad speeds on the highway are subsequently being sold for scrap next week as total write-offs. Don't envy them just yet. Keep your car in control. It's a long drive— your career—it's not a race to the next petrol pump. Let others win for half an hour. Big deal. Enjoy the music, stress less.

There's no deficit of opinion, theory, advice when it comes to handling the initial years at work. I think there's an abundance of it, actually, which doesn't help. S. Radhakrishnan wrote at a point in his commentary on the Bhagavad Gita (while commenting on IV:17):

> What is the right course is not generally obvious. The ideas of our time, the prescriptions of traditions, the voice of conscience get mixed up and confuse us. In the midst of this, the wise man seeks a way out by a reference to immutable truths…

What is the *right course* at the workplace, as we navigate the initial years of our chosen tracks, is also generally not obvious. Varying interpretations of morality, assorted and conflicting advice from buddies and friends and godmothers, and a hundred other things all make it difficult for us to make our choices. I'm attempting to get a sense of the *immutable truths* of work—the way my limited intellect understands them. Those basics are what I—a middle-aged, middle-management level guy who punches his card every morning at the workplace and attends meetings and replies to mails and dissects his annual increment with a calculator—attempt to bring to you here. I have no billion-dollar turnovers, no string of published works, no philosophical halo of a *guru*.

But I want answers, and I've tried to share what I found with you in this.

Read it, therefore. It may give you a few of yours.

PART I

1

I'm not senior enough for me to need to read managerial claptrap right now. Or am I?

Most people I know cringe at the thought of *management books* even more than they cringe at *self-help* stuff. From what little I understand, it is primarily because: (a) they all tend to use language which is apparently coded in a way that only MBAs are supposed to get what they say, and (b) far too many things written are about really rich and famous people. If I'm not running a billion-dollar group, does understanding how Sony or Iacocca or Jack Welch run their systems have any immediate application to my significantly less glamorous life, where there's often a lot of month left at the end of the salary?

So, if you're:

- neither an MBA nor an expert in *management*,
- not really rich enough to quite be able to instantly implement and replicate what Bill Gates, Warren Buffet or Steve Jobs did while working,
- not having a team of 300 reporting in to you for you to practice your leadership or thought skills in the flamboyant laboratory that is the workplace,

do you still need to read any philosophy about how to live, for want of a better phrase, your work life? More importantly, do you *want* to? Is this relevant to you if you're 24 and your workspace is no more than your cluttered workstation? Is this relevant to you if nobody reports in to you, and you don't fill any appraisal forms? Is this relevant to you if your salary account isn't enough to draw the attention of any tax authority on the planet?

Yes, it is.

If you don't understand *how* work happens, how life fundamentally operates, you will possibly end up spending years and years as a whiner, and then years and years as a brooding cynic whose true talent the world never appreciated.

Like, seriously, what a waste.

Also, with that approach, you'll always remain too junior to need to understand any *fundas*. So, it's a self-fulfilling cycle.

- Stage 1: I'm too junior, so I don't have to bother about all this.
- Stage 2: I didn't bother about all this, so I stayed too junior.

No matter *how* many times you tell yourself 'I'm not so ambitious', you don't really want this to be the closing thought of your career, do you?

If you're so decidedly *not ambitious*, maybe you shouldn't take up a career in the first place. Spare everyone the drama and the trauma. To start a career with 'let's see, I'm not *really* ambitious' as the underlying sentiment is to wait to fail from day one. You may as well tell yourself 'I'm not *so* interested in him', and then turn up for your wedding with him. What's the point? Where is this going to end?

Your ambition may not be material; you may not be obsessively ambitious in terms of the pompous visiting card or being chauffeur driven in an S-Class Merc. You may not want to cut people's throats or date the proprietor's relatives to rise up the ladder. That's perfectly OK. But you can't *not* be ambitious about making a reputation. When I say *ambition*, it's not about people clapping for you. It's fundamentally about self-respect. It's about leaving noticeable vacuums behind when you move on—from a task, from a system or from the planet itself. Yes, we're all finally dispensable, but it's about making sure that the shoes you wear aren't *too* easy to be filled in by the next guy who steps into them.

If you said, 'I'm OK with 50 per cent marks in the boards, it doesn't matter anyway' to yourself, was it genuinely about a lack of ambition—you'd risen above all material success and become non-attached—or was it that you simply couldn't be bothered to slog hard enough to do more? Ask yourself if your supposed state of detached bliss is really that—or is it that you are just too lazy, disorganised and laidback? 'What's the point of me doing all this; boss will finally promote that lackey anyway?' could mean just that, or it could be the secret code for 'I'm not going to compromise on my leisure/socialising/whatever—let these poor sods with nothing else to do in life pretend that work is all that matters. PS—I can't beat them at work anyway.' Make sure that at least *you* know which of the two it actually is. Don't tell yourself that the professional grapes are sour because you can't stretch yourself enough to reach them. Everyone tells the odd untruth at office once in a while—but why lie to yourself? There are enough people out there to make a fool of you anyway; don't add yourself to the list.

We live in an era where everyone wants to be *different*. Where being offbeat is celebrated, sometimes excessively so. Where every other person now tells us he'd rather be a DJ or a designer or a hip-hop artist than a lawyer, engineer, doctor or bureaucrat. Which is, of course, brilliant. Three cheers to it. But it's also very handy for not wanting to attend classes in college and for being very quickly bored at work. Everyone who has limited interest in working hard can't explain it away with the convenient argument of not being interested in *conventional* work and answering only to the call of their hidden talents, which can sometimes be too well hidden. The dismissiveness towards the solidity of basic, grounded, *fundas*-clear work and the fascination for being a rockstar by strength of personality alone can lead to castles being made on very shaky foundations.

I think any relatively junior/young professional, who makes the mistake of not investing time and energy in getting his fundamentals sorted, is switching on a mental time bomb's timer switch. At some point in the future, the damn thing will blow up in your face.

The specifics of my religious practices may differ from someone else's, but that is not my obsession. I have to sort myself as a philosopher first. The specifics of my company's work culture may differ from its competitor's—but I need to sort myself as a person and as a professional, first. Cut out your religion, your gender, your academic pedigree—nothing is more irritating than the endless flaunting of where you gathered your education and implicitly your intellectual superiority over the rest of us, incidentally—and cut out the jazz about your work stream's or your company's *style* of functioning. Get a sense of what you are, without all those tags. Sort yourself. Work on yourself. Work on finding *your* True North. Work on understanding your expectations from yourself. Work on understanding the overall atmosphere in which you exist, personally and professionally—the very basics. Your teachers in school gave you the overall reference points: man is so many years old on the planet, we have so many elements, we have the atmosphere above and the earth's crust below, the moon around us and the other planets at this distance, this is how the sun is. They taught you, for example, that it is not the sun that rises and goes down, it's you who is rotating on the earth's surface and sees it that way. You need to understand the basics of how work happens *that* way. It'll be fundamental to how you see the things that happen around you as you live through the initial years. It'll be fundamental to how you respond to them.

Plato spoke of the philosopher king. I'd want to emphasise the need for the emergence of the philosopher–worker.

But is that too far-fetched an idea?

My limited understanding is that irrespective of whether you are a graduate in English Hons or a PhD in Mechanical Engineering, no academic background or intellectual expertise in a domain area will suffice to keep sanity, peace of mind and emotional stability intact once you are in a workplace, unless you have acquired a broader vision of things. A master's degree in shipping management has never helped anyone combat seasickness when the waves begin to toss you around, has it? When your plane is on fire and about to crash land, your temperament is likely to be tested far more than your aeronautical skills. When the economy is struggling and your organisation is cutting your CTC or cutting your best office friend's name from the rolls altogether, you cannot resolve that question with a PPT. Whatever skills you acquire—software programming, soldiering, surgery, editing, acting, whatever—the questions you think about while driving home at the end of the day are unlikely to be about specifics of programmes or scripts or medical journals. They are far more likely to be about natural justice, fair opportunities, hostile lobbies, complicated bosses, perceived prejudice, loving and detestable colleagues, how far you've come and where you want to go from here. They are far more likely to be thoughts about clarity and satisfaction, and a sense of belonging and happiness, of recognition and of achievement or of the depressing lack of all that.

So *juniority*, for lack of a more legitimate dictionary word, is not going to keep you insulated from *all this* any more than being a vegetarian is going to keep you safe if you fall into alligator-infested waters from that seasickness-inducing ship's deck. The alligator will try to chew you up irrespective of whether you eat alligator meat or not. Actually, it's smarter to get out of the *junior* bracket ASAP so that at least you have a higher payslip and a cabin of yours to hide yourself in, without someone peering over from the next cubicle to ask, 'Are you all right?' in that irritating tone when they clearly can make out that you aren't all right and you have no interest in filling them in with the details of what's got you that way. Who wants to repeat verbatim the insults suffered in the boss's cabin, right?

If you are a relative *junior* in the hierarchy of age, and therefore of years of experience, that's not something you could have done anything about. If you are, on that account, also comfortable being a *junior* in terms of how good you are at what you do, and—more importantly—how sorted you are in the head while doing it; that's completely something you *could* have done something about, but opted not to.

When you huddle in the cafeterias and the corridors and the smoke joints and fume at and bitch about them—the supervisor, the sub-boss, the boss, the boss's boss—and derive your satisfaction from abusing them and giggling away, that's a very hollow victory. By mentally accepting the *us*—those who bitch—and *them*—those who are bitched about—you've further strengthened your self-impression that you're fit only to stay on this side of the divide. Do not make the fairly frequent mistake of mentally playing Union versus Management. You're not working in a coal mine or in a chronic loss-making factory in CPM-ruled Bengal. Obstruction and screaming at the management cannot be your *primary* professional target. Instead of laughing at how badly *they* do the job of leading or supervising you, perhaps you need to make this dissection of *them* a learning, rather than an amusing or a frustrating experience. Every bad leader you get is a first-hand teacher right in front of your face, telling you live and real time what *not* to do the day you have to lead teams and people. See what they do. If you think it's crazy, don't giggle and then get back to the daily drudgery—ask yourself how *you* would do it differently. If you don't know the answer to that, then you have no business to be smirking in the first place. If you do find the answer to that, it will do more to shape you into a leader than that IIM-A qualification would. That's OK. Eklavya had no recognised degree in archery, the last I heard.

Laughing at the boss or sticking pins into a voodoo doll of the boss will not, in most cases, make you the boss. And even if you become the boss, these qualifications won't be good enough to make you last. What *will* make you the boss *and* let you last as the boss is bettering your boss—not spending evenings nursing your drink and listing out all the reasons why he/she shouldn't be in that role. So get that *junior* syndrome out of your head and work to understand how seniority is mostly about what you can deliver, not about how many candles your birthday cake has. Your class fellow has 750 Facebook friends and that's fab, but you could find 50 people reporting to you a more interesting option, perhaps? It's not as fun, though—good looking DPs don't help at all and almost nothing you do is *liked*. And yes, what a tragedy—you're working when they are spending five consecutive evenings celebrating their third cousin's wedding which, of course, they *had* to attend. The groom and bride apparently had signed an affidavit saying the marriage will not be legally valid till they have danced for seven hours celebrating it. You're not as indispensable, apparently? Sad. You're attending a stupid *course* instead of going on that vacation with *chacha, chachi, mausa* and that hot cousin twice removed who has a secret crush on you? Tragic. 'You've changed so much', right? Now you don't care for anyone anymore. Tsk, tsk. Ah, the emotional price of attempting to make something of ourselves which is not dependent on our DNA or our company's delegated glory. Choices, choices.

Anyway, I ramble. The basic point of this chapter was: Do you even need to read stuff like this when you're not senior enough to have to look at managerial claptrap? My answer to this is that you absolutely must—since you have the longest career and hopefully a longer life ahead of you at this stage of life, *you have the most to lose* by veering off-track as well. To say it's not as important right now is as stupid as saying that you don't need to check the course on which your ship is sailing, since you've just started the voyage. If you go five degrees off course as you start the voyage, you'll be hundreds of miles off your supposed route when you finally do decide to check your bearings a week later. A bullet fired with a barrel deviating half an inch at the point of firing will end up missing its target by a couple of yards. When Armstrong is being shot off to the moon, the trajectory of the launch going a couple of degrees here or there will decide if he ever lands on the moon or ever gets back here. The consequences of the lack of direction at the outset are so magnified in the long run that you *have* to pay more attention to it when you start. Later, you can philosophise and take deep breaths, but you can't roll time back.

Escaping gravity is a complex effort but once you *have* escaped it, you float a lot easier. We have to learn to handle the accelerated G that a career take-off requires, so that we can go beyond the daily pull of the surface and establish ourselves in a reasonably stable orbit where we're pulled down with much less force. At least to begin with. Then, a different set of battles emerges, but you don't need to learn about handling turbulence till you've learnt to first get the damned plane off the ground, right?

Have you seen *Elysium*? The ruling elite set up a separate orbiting space station, a sort of a mini-planet, and inhabit an easier world, away from overcrowded, chaotic earth. That's what you can do by being the philosopher–worker;

live in a different mental world. One advantageous side effect is that usually you do better work that way, and unless destiny really has a lot of bad karma from previous lives which you need to work your way out of, you end up with relatively relevant and interesting, even if not powerful, work roles. The point is about getting off the overcrowded areas into the more rarefied worlds. We all have to begin our journey in the overcrowded milieu—but taking off, making our way out of it is in our hands.

I don't mean to quote religion at every step, but I read this in the introductory essay to S. Radhakrishnan's commentary on the Bhagavad Gita some 20 years back, and it has stayed with me since then:

> Life is like a game of bridge...We did not invent the game or design the cards. We did not frame the rules and we cannot control the dealing. To that extent, determinism rules. But we can play the game well or play it badly. A skillful player may have a poor hand and yet win the game. A bad player may have a good hand and yet make a mess of it. Our life is a mixture of necessity and freedom, chance and choice. By exercising our choice properly, we can control steadily all the elements and perhaps eliminate altogether the determinism of nature.

The question is not whether you're senior enough to take the game seriously or not. The game's begun. The question is whether you want to play it well right from the first round. The cards, my dear, have already been dealt.

2

The very, very stock exchange of workplace *gyaan*

The basic points I am attempting to make in this chapter are:

- Don't plan your career over lunch with friends; don't seek *gyaan* from everyone.
- Don't be in a hurry to give *gyaan* either till you know what you're talking about.

To many young people, the workplace offers a new emotional challenge every week. And often the first person they turn to for advice is a compatriot, perhaps placed exactly as they are, professionally and emotionally. The *gyaan* dispensed by him/her in all good faith, unto-death bonding and immensely deep love for the best friend is often good enough to derail the friend's career for good for the next couple of years, since the blind leading the blind, no matter how sentimentally, is not a model for great navigation. This is one side of it.

The other side is of those of us holding (what we assume to be) leadership positions beginning to look at ourselves as mentors, patrons, whatever, and beginning to go out of our way to impart career *gyaan* when perhaps we ourselves haven't found most of our answers yet, or when we make the mistake of tutoring or guiding a recipient who probably doesn't want to see our face for one minute more than is absolutely essential. This is something you have to endure with your offspring, perhaps, but there's no need to become daddy to your work juniors and dish out advice when it's clearly both unsolicited and unwelcome. Silence is a not-so-apparent option which we can exercise, too, lest we end up repeating the futile exercise of the teenage rebel being lectured by a grandmom, with neither party gaining anything.

The 20-something walks into his/her new office and, perfectly justifiably, begins to look for social associations and equations just the way he/she looked for a group of friends when he/she walked into a new school or on the first day of college. This is natural. The colleague who shares his/her lunch with you, waits to walk with you to the cafeteria or perhaps drops you home becomes that warm fire in a cold alien landscape, where you want to go to escape the occasional social chill of a place where nobody knows you well enough yet. That's fine. That's fundamental. Nobody's arguing against personal bonding at the workplace.

What's equally fundamental is the fact that the warm, cheery girl on the workstation next to you is not necessarily the best judge of how you are working because you love the food her mother cooks or because she thinks your nail polish shade is fab, while everyone else is asking if you've gone colour blind. Affection does not necessarily equal solidarity. Solidarity does not give someone the *competence* to become your primary advisor, professionally. In reverse, in fact, your newly discovered friends may well give you worse feedback than a non-friend would because it's coloured by the equation and by the unwritten expectation of standing by each other when under fire, from the boss or from others. When Pakistani troops are firing at our soldiers on the border, we aren't really interested in whether, sometimes, the breach of ceasefire or a crossing of the LoC is by *our* men, do we? Hell, no! We have to display solidarity. Solidarity in the office gang means the gang buddies not telling you that it was your mistake, ever. It also, therefore, means you never correcting your mistakes till it's too late to do anything about them anymore. The batsman who displays solidarity with his buddy by never questioning his judgement, never sending him back even when the single is non-existent, will sooner or later run himself or his buddy out. Many a loner has built a stable, sustained, successful career since he/she had no friends to egg him/her on to continue to make a complete ass of himself/herself when he/she was doing stuff patently wrong.

Think about it. You are, perhaps, raw in that system or in that work area. You're not yet placed to judge if your newly discovered BFF is himself/herself a 9/10 professionally. You don't ask your BF/GF for advice on playing the guitar or bowling better leg spin, howsoever much you may love them. You go to someone who can play the guitar or bowl good leg spin. Don't, therefore, seek advice on handling your tasks, projects, people skills or deadlines from your best buddy. Before you know it, unless you are exceptionally lucky in your first calls about people or have a hyperactive guardian angel, your positions will become an extension or perhaps even a reflection of your buddy's. Which will either make you appear like a chicken who has just found a mother hen's wing to take shelter under, or if your buddy is seen as a defiant obstructionist as a new recruit brainwashed to the cause of jihad by an experienced militant.

Love and competence need not overlap. I love my daughters dearly, but asking them for advice on how to run my work affairs is not love, it's straightforward idiocy. You have the right to love your colleague more than your soul sister, but let's have a reality check—Is she professionally qualified or competent or experienced to give you feedback on what course of action to take?

We're all in it together is a great reflex—however, we would do well to remember that it is found in lemmings, too. And by the rats who were *all in it together* as they followed the Pied Piper. The sentiment of solidarity is excellent—but do keep it for where it is relevant, where it is applicable. Honest feedback from a not-so-gushy associate will do more for you than a hanky from a loved one to wipe your angst-filled tears.

Brotherhoods, sisterhoods and standing by your BF/GF no matter what sort of a royal, incompetent mess he/she makes at work is so, so sweet. It is also so utterly stupid. By the time the object of your affection realises that gushy hugs do not make an effective career, he/she will have missed the phase of his/her career where this basic would have made a difference.

The phenomenon of the 'work spouse' has been the subject of much attention. What is less frequently commented on is the work brother, the work sister and the work mother. Dispensing advice, holding hands, providing ample shoulders to rest and cry on and backing every rant of yours against the establishment, these work relations are the perfect emotional support system—and also the perfect way to possibly ruin your career even before it takes off.

I think the work spouse exists, but it doesn't really impact workplaces too deeply, since in an overly politically correct world, people are careful to not be accused of bias, of being sugar daddies or worse. We are wary of being seen to lean too much on work advice or support from someone of the opposite gender, for fear of triggering off gossip that there is *more to it*. In recent years, instances, such as those involving Phaneesh Murthy, David Davidar, etc., have reminded us that proximity to work colleagues can backfire, and so there are built-in warning signals at work, in our heads. No such defensive hesitation exists in the aggressive bro/sis bondings at the workplace, though.

The workplace rant is catharsis, right? But if the rant is not also about what you can *do*—it's nothing more than the *nanad-devrani* gossip about the mother-in-law in TV soaps. It doesn't help.

Chat if you will. But don't, don't make the chat and rant session the basis on which you take work calls. That's really, really underselling yourself.

PART II

3

What am I doing here? I was meant for greater things

I still remember something said in the course of a chat that I had many, many years ago with a cousin of mine who was, at that point of time, a captain in the army, posted in J&K. He was narrating a conversation that had taken place in his officers' mess the previous night. A couple of colleagues of his had some extended and sharp views on the way a General Officer Commanding (GOC) had been handling some issues relating to troops engaged in anti-militancy operations in the state. 'After some time, I couldn't resist it anymore,' 'my cousin said amidst chuckles, 'And I said to X, you know, dear, you have this mess to run and some six people to manage, and seeing how this place has a new problem every third day and dinner is never served on time, no offence, I'd like to see how you run a 10-member team efficiently and not have the kitchen run out of potatoes so often before paying too much attention to your views on how a General should be running a Division.'

That conversation came back to me so many times over the years. I thought of it when I sat in a crowded sleeper class compartment, and heard the group playing cards on the berth above dissect how the government didn't know its job. I thought of it when auto drivers with dysfunctional metres gave me extended *gyaan* while waiting at red lights on how matters of the economy ought to be managed. When I had a semblance of a career, I thought of it often when I heard people complain about *things* not being *handled* well—people who had nothing to do with the word *handle* at any point except when they grasped the one on their bike to come to office. And I would always go back to the mess-GOC conversation and quickly suppress a sarcastic smile, lest someone's sense of self-importance be hurt.

My obsession with reading about matters military has inflicted many parallels from that field

on the younger lot who have had to endure working with me at different points of time. On many
occasions, especially among young joinees in
the last few years, a lot of people have opinions
on how systems ought to be run, on how industries should operate, on where, for instance, is
the media heading. And I have sometimes come
back to them with a basic point: That their point
of view on how the generals are running an army
will carry greater weight if they can master their
basic skills as soldiers or officers, wherever
they be placed at that point of time. I am a little cynical about someone who can't carry off
his uniform or shoot straight having a point of
view on the management of troops or someone
who can't hit a ball with the middle of the bat
having a view on how the cricket team's coach
should have used his resources. I am, therefore,
inclined towards paying relatively less attention
to, for instance, a journalist who cannot make a
page without half-a-dozen grammatical errors or
a reporter who can't break a single story before
competition, having the leisure to discuss the
way the media is heading over extended cafeteria conversations. I'm not saying they don't have
a right—everyone has the right to have an opinion. But equally, everyone else has an equal—or

greater—right to ignore their opinion. I can have an opinion about Obama's healthcare plans—but the fact remains that I know jack about health care, insurance or American society's views on it, so it's not as if my opinion should count for anything. As Hubert H. Humphrey so bluntly—and accurately—puts it, 'The right to be heard does not automatically include the right to be taken seriously.'[1]

To be taken seriously, we have to be serious about what we do—at that given point of time. And take that chip off our shoulder which tells the world that *given a chance* at that more important task in the future, we will let it know how amazing we are. That's not really how it works. You can't be an indifferent lieutenant and keep your military skills a well-guarded secret till they make you a lieutenant general because you'll probably retire as a major. You can't bat sleepily in Ranji Trophy matches and keep your best batting for when you are the team India captain, playing at Lords—because you won't ever get into team India that way. You can't mess up basic work as a sub-editor in a newspaper and wait to play a real life *The Devil Wears Prada* role since the devil is also bloody competent at what she does.

Don't get me wrong—I am not discussing competence here. If someone is fundamentally incompetent for a type of job or is fundamentally incompetent, period, then this book isn't for them; neither is any other. I am assuming a basic minimum level of competence, interest and skill in anyone who picks up something to read which is addressing fundamental questions of how to survive and grow in the jungle that is the workplace.

And when people with fairly decent skills and competence do below-par work on a consistent basis, it is, increasingly enough, because somewhere in their mind, they are bored. They're saying to themselves: This isn't what I came for! They want bigger, smarter stuff to do. The problem is that their disinterest in doing well the boring, insignificant stuff in hand becomes the biggest handicap in anyone daring to entrust them with bigger, smarter stuff.

This may well be a generalisation and not applicable for perhaps 70 per cent of young workers, but the flip side of the increased sense of confidence in Gen-Y is that far too many people assume that they know a little more than they actually do. The point of *being confident* is often drilled into minds to the degree that cockiness is seen as aspirational; *believe in yourself* can get distorted into the mindset that keeping your head down and acknowledging that you don't know something well enough is a trait for small-town losers only. Too many people starting off their careers—even when they're yet to establish a track record of competence or dependability—tend to react to *smaller* tasks with a raised eyebrow or shoot off a mail which ambiguously asks, 'Am I supposed to do *that*?' with an unwritten PS saying 'But this is not what I joined up for, really?' By doing that small, inconsequential task with a reluctant, disinterested state of mind—and therefore doing it badly, usually—they send out the message that either they're too stuck up to get their hands dirty when required or—more often—that they're not good enough to even handle that small a task without getting it wrong. And thereby starts the familiar tale of *that place didn't do full justice to my talent.* Er, even if justice is infrequent, it could also be that perhaps, you kept your talent rather well hidden, you know?

This topic lends itself to many fun quotes, but one of my favourites is this one by Sam Ewing: 'Hard work spotlights the character of people:

some turn up their sleeves, some turn up their noses, and some don't turn up at all.'[2]

In many cases, what the immediate team, the manager, the supervisor is seeing as basic hard work is being seen as *trivial* by the one asked to do it, and that difference of perspective can often be a deal-breaker in a sense. Any relatively young/junior employee can inflict no greater damage to his/her reputation than being seen to be one of those who turn up their noses or don't turn up at all. Most teams will far more easily bear with a not-so-smart person who is trying to work hard, than with an over smart individual who displays disdain and sends the vibes that the stuff coming his/her way is beneath him/her.

In the teams I have worked with, I have always, by reflex, valued slightly greater the people who can do even the relatively tedious, boring, non-glamorous tasks well—the tasks for which there are no volunteers—without incessant whining. For the glamorous, fun tasks, you will always have a plethora of volunteers. But behind every pilot flying a fighter jet, there are a dozen people going over his plane in a pre-flight check, the thoroughness of which ensures that he lands back alive and in one piece. If those dozen tech guys don't do their job, you don't have the fancy pilot anymore pretty soon—you just have a dead pilot. Even the pilot has to spend hours and hours on a simulator before he can fly fancy loops in the sky—he can't dismiss it as tedious and boring. If he does, he's never going to get to fly the actual stuff. You can't run an air force if everyone joins up only to fly the jets and you can't run teams if basic, everyday work is done with disinterest and disdain—that system is guaranteed to crash.

An SRK wouldn't have been an SRK today if he hadn't caught our attention with his television debut in *Fauji*. He didn't have a producer or an actor dad to launch him as a lead in 70 mm. But if he had turned up his nose at being part of a multicast TV serial, he'd have joined the league of hundreds whose careers stayed and stopped there. A Karan Johar will have to slog as an assistant director to get a hang of the system, even if he is from a cine family. So will an Aamir Khan. A Sachin will have to, in his initial days, learn to focus even if his job in a given match may be no more than accompanying the drinks tray. Golf has no deficit of stories of caddies who learnt the nuances of the game while lugging around the clubs of more affluent players who approached the game in a more leisurely fashion, and then made more money than them by mastering the game.

The first newspaper I worked for sold just a handful of copies in Jammu. There was no prestige, no power and practically no money. I had no clear career plan at that point. It was just by reflex that *whatever* came my way in that comparatively derelict office, I did it as well as I could. For a phase, I was assigned what was largely seen, even in that relatively inconsequential power hierarchy, as the most inconsequential page in terms of content. I ignored the deliberate slight by the people who ran it at that point, and did all I could to make it look the most interesting page of the paper, even if nobody read it. I learnt the basics of layout, so the disinterest of the design team in handling that irrelevant part of the paper didn't impact how that page looked. I put in twice the hours required to master the fundamentals by trial and error. As I put up the final page one day, the designer who was making the infinitely more prestigious page one with a more senior colleague stopped to look at my handiwork, nodded appreciatively and gave me a life lesson: '*Aise hi* page *banaate rahoge to ek din iss* paper *ka* page one *pakka banaoge.*'

He was right. I did make the page one of that paper. I did more than that, actually; I became its editor. And when I moved out of J&K, I carried those lessons. I never made the egoistic mistake of assuming that the work from which on any given day I earned my daily bread was beneath me—because unless I did it well, I would never master doing better, greater, more visible work. On multiple occasions, be it the assignment I was given or the city I was sent to, people sympathised with me and said, 'What are you doing here? You should have been given X or Y.' I ignored their sympathy and their predictions of my fading into obscurity and worked to deliver the best I could in the circumstances I was placed in.

And I read and re-read what Vivekananda had written, for in those years my managerial basics were less evolved and for all doubts I would go back to the monk. I put this up in large fonts in front of my workstation for years and years so I wouldn't crib—or even if I did crib, I wouldn't allow that to reflect in the manner in which I did whatever my work at that point was:

By doing well the duty which is nearest to us, the duty which is in our hands now, we make ourselves stronger

… We find ourselves in the position for which we are
fit, and if one has some capacity above another, the
world will find it out too … He who grumbles at the little
thing that has fallen to his lot to do, will grumble at everything. Always grumbling, he will lead a miserable life.
But that man who does his duty as he goes, putting his
shoulder to the wheel, higher and higher duties will fall
to his share.

I had many little things that fell to my lot.
When I see kids who start their careers on day
one with very big brands in very big cities and
then treat work as something they have to sort of
fit in between sorting the current complications
of their personal life or as something that they
have to make an effort to focus on, I'm often left
stunned at the sheer audacity. Maybe it's a small-
town mindset. But when I see the *paan* shop
wallah spend a minute as he closes the shutters
on mumbling his prayers and putting his head on
the window, I get that sentiment. Respect what
you do, do it well, period. What's *small* work?
There is no dearth of *paanwallah*s in Delhi, who,
by doing what they do well, probably earn four
times what I do after 20 years of slogging it out
as a journalist.

Vivekananda has it spot on, I think. The one
who grumbles, always grumbles, and nothing is

good enough for the grumbler. Beyond a point, most teams and bosses stop paying attention. Perry M. Smith uses an interesting phrase for that breed: the chronic malcontents.[3] I know there isn't too much justice in the real world, and often we are dealt a raw deal, but in response to that, doing what you have in hand *today* badly and with disinterest is *not* the answer to a career problem, ever.

You have to remember the basic: Do your duty as you go. Do the work in your hand *now* to the best of your ability, always and every time. The rest will follow of its own accord.

Notes

1. See http://www.britannica.com/topic/276362/supplemental-information. Retrieved on 16 September 2014.
2. Branch, Trevior. (2011). *The Drama-Free Workweek: How to Manage Difficult People for Workplace and Career Success*. USA: Trafford Publishing.
3. Smith, Perry M. (1998). *How to Run an Organization Successfully: Rules & Tools for Leaders—A Down-to-Earth Guide to Effective Managing*. New York: Avery Publishing Group.

4

Yes, you're clearly better than the imbecile who got promoted. Now?

I'm going to be a little impractical here.

I'm going to ask you to not grudge that colleague's promotion ahead of you—that promotion which you very clearly think is a factor of PR skills or a very good phase in his planetary chart, since there's no other reason you can think of for such a bizarre occurrence. I'm asking you to ignore it altogether, not spend a minute cursing your bad luck or abusing the system. OK, maybe a bit of the latter—one does need to let off steam sometimes.

But the way I see it—if you really think someone is not good enough for a position they have been elevated to—then *their being promoted to it is the best thing to happen to you.* Fundamentally, there's absolutely no injustice coming your way.

There are three ways this can go from here:

- He/she will turn out to be essentially unfit for the post gifted. Power corrupts, and higher positions magnify both strengths and weaknesses. If there are fundamental skews, they will now become more visible to everyone, and what was just your opinion will become public knowledge. The stint will totter and after a point of time, lean over and collapse, leaving many more people with an insight into the risk of giving such a person the edge ahead of you the next time.

- You will see that he/she is actually pretty good at the task he/she is doing, and the only way for you to get ahead is to be even better than he/she is now. He/she will turn out to be actually capable of more than you thought and will begin to evolve and adapt and show maturity, perhaps even earn your grudging respect. Your option then could be, perhaps, to show maturity in your responses, try to crack the code which put this individual ahead of you in the career race and match—or beat—them fair and square by investing in yourself and competing on a level playing field. If the system that rewarded him has actually been logical and reasonably fair, you'll earn your rewards, too, in all probability.

- You will realise that the structure and the person are both working in a loop that is utterly loony and beyond your comprehension that you want to neither emulate nor tolerate, and you'll start investing in yourself so that you can find validation and respect outside your immediate system. You'll work on yourself, driven by the urge to show them, through appreciation and growth elsewhere, what you were worth. You will get going, and driven by sheer angst, jealousy, irritation—all of which are very good motivators, trust me—you will end up becoming a far better professional than you originally were, irrespective of whether you win that micro office-rank battle or not. It may take you a while, it won't happen in a fortnight, but then revenge is a dish best served cold, isn't it?

All three are essentially win-win situations that shake you out of any complacency that you may have been stuck with. So, I'd suggest you don't see it as a stroke of bad luck. More often than not, it'll be a blessing in disguise.

Had they just stayed where they were, you would have had the satisfaction of assuming that they aren't good enough for bigger things, while they would have had the luxury to whine and say luck wasn't with them, they didn't suck up to the boss, etc., (*whereas, by implication, you did*) and that if they had been given a chance at bigger things, they'd have changed the world. And you couldn't have divested them of their halo of martyrdom. I mean, how do you counter-argue with Kejriwal about what he *could* have done in Delhi if he'd lasted longer? And you would have been content to be better than just where you are. So them—*the Undeserving*—being promoted ahead of you is what leaves you better placed, any which way.

This may seem too good-goody or naïve, but over the 20 odd years of my career, I have acquired even stronger faith in option 1, which comes back not from social or economic analysis, but from Vivekananda, again. He wrote something which I think has stood the test of time, at all levels of work:

No man can long occupy satisfactorily a position for which he is not fit. By doing well the duty which is nearest to us, the duty which is in our hands now, we make ourselves stronger; and improving our strength in this manner we may even reach a state in which it shall be our privilege to do the most coveted and honoured duties in life and in society. (Chaturvedi, emphasis added)

For years and years, we have grown to believe that networks, contacts, connections help people get ahead. We envy people's luck, situations, DNA. We look at all the core areas of our country—in the media, we typically say that India is obsessed with politics, cricket and Bollywood—and bemoan that just as it happens there, people get ahead when they don't deserve to.

For years and years, I have seen faces come and go in these glamorous domains, and wondered at the phenomenal accuracy of Vivekananda's managerial take on the guy who is going too fast, overtaking you—and I've come to genuinely believe that No Man—including, and starting with, me—can long occupy satisfactorily a position for which he is not fit.

The keyword, of course, is *long*. And our impatience often explodes at the mere fact of someone occupying a position for which he/

she—in our opinion—is not fit. We don't have the patience to see whether that person will last, whether he/she will have the temperament and ability to reinvent himself/herself. We fret, fume, sometimes vocally. Often in all of that, we make ourselves look like sore losers and further damage our prospects of getting ahead as and when circumstances turn more congenial.

Apart from battling and resolving my own moments of angst on this issue from 25 to 40, the reason I have attempted to resolve it in my head and found it a recurrent track is that often the single biggest office friendship breaker is someone's elevation from within a peer group. I've seen that from the time I was made the senior under officer in an NCC camp—which frosted my equation with those whom I was sharing a tent with, in frosty conditions anyway—to when I promote people in my teams today. Second, there's massive resentment when someone perceived to be not good enough gets a role/position above others; the ones left waste more energy in being frustrated and bitching than in countering with better work. My argument is that *getting a position means absolutely nothing except a speedy descent or constant mockery if someone isn't cut out for that role*, and so there's no sense in being jealous on the grounds that they aren't good enough. A Deve Gowda or a Chandrashekhar or an I.K. Gujral can become the prime minister, with all due regards, and even if anyone's sentiments are being hurt, it makes no profound difference. They're unlikely to be studied in history books.

Manmohan Singh has said that history will be kinder to him than contemporary media has; we'll have to wait for that history to be written to see how that works out, but you get the general picture. No one—simply no one—can 'long occupy *satisfactorily* a position for which he is not fit.' Believe in Karma; yes, it bites back. Have the patience to see. Either he is not fit, and will not grow there, having attained his level of incompetence (*that phrase is from The Peter Principle; more on that later in the book*). Or he *is* good enough, in which case understand that you're just being envious and start matching up with work. When Indira Gandhi was first chosen to be the candidate for prime minister, I believe the phrase among the Congress biggies was *goongi gudiya*. And *that*, as events proved, she most certainly was not!

When my career drifted to smaller cities at different points of time and then drifted to bigger cities too, and I waited a year, then two, then three, for things to make any sense, I sold the situation to myself—pretty good salesmanship, I thought—by tacking up Confucius on the board at my workstation. What did the scholar say? This: 'Do not be desirous of having things done quickly. Do not look at small advantages. The desire to have things done quickly prevents their being done thoroughly. Looking at small advantages prevents great affairs from being accomplished.'

I was clear my life was going to be a great affair. So I magnanimously left off gnawing my nails over small advantages. And given the months I have made my publishers wait for the first draft of this motley collection of personalised takes, it's evident that I have successfully conquered the base instinct to have things done quickly as well. Vivekananda used a phrase in a letter with which I used to sell even more patience to myself when things didn't go my way—'no indecent haste!' That sounded nice. Am I missing the corporate bus? Am I getting older and getting nowhere? Where's my Merc, my six-pack, my penthouse office? Ah, I told myself regally, with no money in my account, 'Don't prevent great affairs from being accomplished, Anshul, and be in no indecent haste.'

I'm still sane—so it probably worked.

A lot of the angst about someone getting more than their due is about who *gives* them that due. A patron, a starry-eyed boss, a sugar daddy or maybe just daddy. But can someone be *made* a star or an anything?

Yes and No.

A lot of No, actually.

I will now list out many of the examples which I recount to those unfortunate enough to have to endure my company when these questions come up in conversation.

When I was in college, Madhuri was *the* rage. I watched bemused, as multiple movies produced by the Kapoors cast Sanjay Kapoor, the brother of Anil and Boney, as the lead opposite Madhuri. It made no damn sense. He wasn't cut out for that. He must have been 10 other great things—but he was not a *star*, he simply could not hold the screen in a frame with Madhuri without saying, 'I don't belong here' in every expression. At some point, I guess all three brothers realised that this won't work and ended the torture inflicted on Sanjay, as well as the audience. I have nothing against him generally; he's done well in the industry in whatever *else* he's attempted, primarily as a producer, to the best of my understanding.

A few months back, I went to see *Besharam*. No movie with Ranbir Kapoor does bad these days, or so common logic goes. Midway through the movie, I tried to understand why the leading lady had been cast in it—*what* was she doing as the heroine opposite the reigning screen stud? I couldn't figure it out. Neither, apparently, could most people. The movie gave Ranbir one of his few clear-cut flops.

Now, there was a 20-year gap between these two, but every single year has brought multiple illustrations of the basic truth: If you *don't* have it in you at that point of time, your papa plonking you up there pretending that you *do* is only going to bring it out before everyone else all that quicker. Harry Baweja cannot make Harman Baweja an overnight superstar simply by casting Priyanka Chopra in his debut film and spending 50 crores to make it. Vashu Bhagnani cannot do it with Jacky, either by launching or by re-launching him incessantly. Mithun Chakraborty cannot make Mimoh a superstar. Ekta cannot make Tusshar a superstar. The Big B's name alone cannot make Abhishek a superstar.

Merely coming from a politically influential family cannot make Riteish Deshmukh a superstar. Being the son of *the* Mukesh cannot make Nitin Mukesh Bollywood's greatest singer, talented though he may be. The list is practically endless.

I have nothing to say about the aggregate skills of these individuals—tomorrow Harry or Tusshar or any other actor who hasn't mastered cinema yet may have a mega million dollar hit, and Abhishek has had some fine performances already, from *Yuva* to *Guru*. The point I am making is that if you think somebody is lucky because today he has been placed *ahead* through connections, networks, relations—hell, there's no reason to be really jealous. Half the time, the big name only makes you the butt of bigger jokes—just ask Uday Chopra about twitter on the day he announced he was retiring from, err, acting. Your daddy—or for that matter your sugar daddy—can have you cast opposite anyone in the biggest movie of the year, but even he can't make that movie work when it comes to people buying tickets. If you can't act, you're going to show that now to a million people on very big theatre screens.

Your patron can perhaps be so powerful as to plonk you into the cricket team, but even he can't ask Australian bowlers to bowl slower at you or for groundsmen there to make slower, easier pitches for you to swing your bat around. So if your middle stump goes cartwheeling, the whole country is going to watch it nine times in slow motion and ask why a c*** like you is in the team in the first place. Your pappa can gift you a supercar, but not driving skills, and you may well end up bashing into expensive Audis at midnight on Mumbai's roads and then give him sleepless nights proving that it wasn't you ever there in the first place, while he has to replace the damaged cars with more expensive ones.

Moral of the story: If you don't deserve it, dude, getting it is going to be a very mixed blessing. So there's no real reason for the rest of us to look at you and take deep, long breaths saying, 'Lucky bastard.' No, not that lucky, actually. And so often, there is no real advantage for those in ostensibly privileged situations. Unknown boys from India's B-cities have come in and amassed millions in the IPL, while I have never heard much of Rohan Gavaskar's career as a cricketer.

After finishing 12th, I jotted down some random career choices. One of them was *prime minister.* By the time I turned 40, not only did I have no chance of ever getting there, but, more importantly, the post had turned so non-aspirational. What place in history did Chandrashekhar, I.K. Gujral or H.D. Deve Gowda manage to carve out by becoming the political leaders of the world's largest democracy? What did Manmohan Singh gain by a decade-long tenure as PM? Was he any happier, any more powerful or any more respected than he would have been, had he retired from the system as Narasimha Rao's finance minister? What exactly did becoming the PM amount to if you become the butt of collective national—and then global—disdain, and only your philosophical rooting keeps you going through the insults and the mockery? What is the point of it? Someone can even make you the PM—just as someone can give you a lead slot in a mega budget film—but even someone powerful enough to make you the PM cannot make people believe in you.

The exultation of getting that movie /getting a slot in the team/becoming a minister or indeed the PM will fade away once it becomes clear whether someone is cut out to deliver that role well or not. All Dhoni's support couldn't make

R.P. Singh or Suresh Raina permanent fixtures in the team. The grand legacy of the Gandhi surname couldn't stop crowds from drifting away during campaigning for the Delhi assembly polls even as Sheila Dixit beseeched crowds—'*arey* Rahul *ji ko to sun jaiye.*'

I've mentioned earlier in this chapter that India is seen to primarily consume three things—Bollywood, Cricket and Politics. From what I've seen over the last decade, across all three, there are more duds who are just floating around propped by influence, connections, relatives, boyfriends, dads than I can count. They have been gifted movies, they have been godfathered in sports, they have been gifted positions from which they could theoretically have become powerful, exceptional, actually worthy of attracting our attention or at least our envy.

But they couldn't.

Too many of these privileged elite make it to twitter trends only when there's a joke on them floating around. Occupying a slot, being gifted a chair, a role, means *nothing* unless you can leave a mark. And that, to my mind, is the point of occupying it *satisfactorily*. If that isn't happening, the holder of that slot deserves your sympathy, not envy. Dole it out, go on.

Vivekananda will of course describe it in the 'No man can long occupy satisfactorily…' tone. In more everyday language, I'd prefer the concept of *the honeymoon period*. It ends. So when we comment on someone in the 'fluke *lag gaya*' tone, let us also remember that flukes—if they are flukes—don't last. Remind yourself: The desire to have things done quickly prevents their being done thoroughly.

Even if you have neither the 'jack' nor the luck to get them done quickly, don't fret; instead, do them thoroughly.

You'll probably laugh last.

5

Career crisis? Come, join the club

As I sit down to write this, today's TOI's *Thought For The Day* quotes Lenin: 'There are decades where nothing happens; and there are weeks where decades happen.'[1]

That's pretty much how it happens in careers, too, so often, even though we could compress *decades* to *years*, since the former would make it a fundamentally depressing thought. But the basic point is valid: our growth in whatever we do, whether in practical terms, such as rank, salary, cabins, or by more esoteric inward benchmarks, such as self-belief, an absence of insecurity and a lack of need of validation by others—it's very rarely linear, straight. There are dips, there are flat lines, there are also unexpected surges. In fact, you have far greater control over how you grow internally—master your fears, develop your skills, earn some respect—than you have over organisational acknowledgements of such growth.

And that's a reality you have to live with unless you want to turn into a brooding cynic within the first decade of your career.

If you are going to work, no matter what system or company you work for, you are at some point going to face a situation which, to your mind, will seem totally unfair, totally illogical and completely screwed up. In fact, the longer you have done good work (or what you see as good work) in that system, the greater will be your angst, since you'll turn around and say, 'After all I've proved, *this* is what I get?'

It's rather theatrical, perhaps, but today, when I speak to someone—and most often that someone will be in the 21–35 age bracket, given how old I've grown now—who is in obvious grief owing to a work situation and apparently facing a totally unfair deal (sometimes with me as primary contributing factor)—I am reminded of the tale where Gautam Buddha asked the grieving mother who came to him for solace to bring a mustard seed from a home which had never seen death. Her grief did not lessen after that futile effort, but she realised that almost everyone has had to face that grief at some point or another. Work, of course, is not life or death—or in some cases it is, the newspapers occasionally tell us about how job pressures or failures actually *have* pushed people off the cliff—but there are very, very few of us who have not faced moments of acute frustration during a decently long stint at doing what we do, no matter how much we think we put into it. This could hold true if you're 25, 30, 35 or 45. It's not a *phase* thing. And yet, the fact that such a situation on a given day is not unique to you, in no way lessens how it impacts you. If a million Indians get injured in accidents each year, it doesn't lessen my trauma when a truck drives right into my car, so I don't mean to say that just because it's a part of almost everyone's life, it's not going to hurt.

There may be no one *right* way to deal with this when it happens. But I do think that there is one clearly wrong way. A combination of a *this is all so screwed up* scene + a sense of things not working out + the system not recognising them + recurrent flak is, over time, sometimes accompanied by a belief that only networks/lobbying/currying favour with the boss/belonging to a particular affiliation, ethnic group, gender, etc. *work* in that system. The battle, in effect, is given up, and a deep sense of angst or cynicism seeps in, replacing the expectations of the joining phase.

Which is perhaps quite justifiable. My problem with this response is that it may well lead to a self-fulfilling prophecy. There's nothing for me here will sooner or later lead to there being actually nothing for you there. And that cycle could well be repeated at the next place—for all you know. The Known Devil is an easier option than the Unknown One. So even if you do take a call to distance yourself, move away, find a new role in the system, find a role in a new organisation— don't do it at the cost of letting the battle scar your basics, or of looking at alignments, equations, personal PR skills as the new reference points for a good work atmosphere. The point that needs to be argued with yourself—and argued intensely—is that there is, actually, nothing to replace the USP of individual character and of the manner in which you do what you do.

We have all lived through the recent stagnant economy years where thousands of people got, in place of increments, *reduced* salaries after doing a decent job. Thousands of reasonably efficient young—and not so young—people in the sectors worst affected by the economic down-turn turned up one not-so-fine day to find that the places they were working for weren't work-ing anymore. That wasn't the result of any office conspiracy or anyone filling the boss's ears with goss about you—that was just the way the dice rolled on a given day. The point is that some-times a career crisis is preventable, sometimes manageable, and sometimes it's just a truck that drives into your stationary car. It happens and we have to learn to deal with it when it hap-pens, so that we're not left with our emotional and temperamental basics all messed up as we resume the journey. X/Y/Z can at best mess up your *job*—but only *you* can mess up your career.

Look around you—who hasn't had a career cri-sis, a phase where whatever they attempted led nowhere? Where was Salman Khan just before the whole Wanted/Ready/Dabangg sequence kicked off? Where was Yuvraj Singh—first in chemo, then out of the team—before com-manding a 14-crore tag in the 2014 IPL? Where was Amitabh Bachchan just before KBC—with a mortgaged residence? Hell, if Apple could ask Steve Jobs to move, what do you expect? Having half the company's shares given to you for putting in your heart and soul into what you did? That's not the way any system works. Why should yours?

Pressure is inevitable. Why are kids in IITs putting a noose around the ceiling fan and kicking the stool from beneath their feet after having a slot in a sure-shot professional line? The career crisis can incapacitate us even before the career starts, if we don't get a sense of perspective. Come into your career looking for ways to learn, to grow, to widen what you can do and understand—to grow intellectually and emotionally. Yes, it sounds stupid, but financially should be the last bit, if you can afford that, in the initial years. A few months back, I forwarded a tweet by Harsha Bhogle to my financially less empowered colleagues, and I don't know if they laughed or cried when they read it, but it's a thought that made sense since it was coming from within an industry where too many young people are making obscene amounts of money far too early: 'When the going gets tough, the best become more valuable. Spend your early years trying to become the best, not necessarily the richest'.

Of course, *early years* is subjective; mine, for instance, are still on.

To scream and rant at the unavoidable—the appointment made by someone who owns the place where you're just a salaried employee, the closure of an office wing, the reallocation of roles by a boss who is clearly not a fan of your work style, the announcement of a freeze in salaries—is the equivalent of honking away at a car that has broken down in your lane.

It's *not* going to move for you, dear, and the sooner you get that, the better. Reverse, and find space to move ahead in another lane. Unless, of course, the economy is totally jacked or the traffic in all lanes has totally stopped moving—then the lane shifting may also be not very productive. Relax, stop revving on the accelerator, listen to music and bide your time till things move on their own, or some other lane becomes navigable. A Delhi, Mumbai or Bangalore driver has to be able to handle long periods of his car going absolutely nowhere if he has to reach anywhere. Air travellers have to get used to hanging about in lounges before boarding. It's OK. Sometimes, that's what you have to do in your career as well. There will be periods when you will not move an inch forward. That means that you're on pause; it doesn't mean that you aren't heading anywhere. You're heading somewhere even when you wait at the airport. Cut yourself some slack when you're in the waiting lounge.

I grew up watching Gavaskar bat and by the time I write this book, Sachin has played 20 years and more, and has retired from the game. In all these years, I have read umpteen times about how Indian batsmen are tigers on flat sub-continental pitches and domesticated kittens on bouncy pitches elsewhere, and of their inability to handle pace on overseas tracks. Gavaskar was the first Indian batsman I watched mastering foreign pacers. As an opener, he inevitably faced the new ball and the freshest bowlers. And he had a fabulous record compared to his peers. One thing he would talk about often was not succumbing to pressure and blindly hitting out to relieve it—stay at the pitch, don't throw your wicket, he would say, and the runs will come. The morning dew will evaporate, the track will ease out, the bowler will tire, you'll be *set* and in the flow. Then, you counter.

A lot of far more flamboyant players have had far shorter-lived careers than Gavaskar's. He stayed at the crease, he stayed in the team; he sold his wicket very, very dearly. I still remember his last Test innings versus Pakistan on a horrible, turning track at the Chinnaswamy stadium, in Bangalore, on the last day of the last match of a five-match Indo-Pak series. The year was 1987;

I was 14 but even today, at 41, I can almost replay it ball by ball. It was a textbook demonstration of what he spoke about. He stayed and stayed, and displayed incredible tenacity and temperament in handling a pitch on which scoring a 50 was quite a task, till given out to a dubious call at 96. India lost the Test by 16 runs, but what happened to the Test seemed almost irrelevant to me at that time.

The only other time I saw something matching that effort was the incredible Eden Gardens Test, during the 2001 Australian tour of India. Anyone who follows cricket will need no reminders of what this is about, of the Test which India won by 171 runs after being forced to follow on, and broke the 16-match winning streak of the Aussies. Day 4 of that Test when Laxman and Dravid put their heads down, and stayed and stayed the whole day without an Indian wicket falling was what that incredible turnaround was based on. India won that match on grit, not flamboyance.

Most of our careers will be won or lost on the same parameters. Learn to play the dot balls. Some jobs can be T20 matches. But careers are Test matches, not T20s. The pitch will ease out, the bowler will tire. Sometimes, staying at the crease is an end in itself. Learn from Gavaskar's basic—if you stay long enough at the crease, take the bouncers that hit you on the helmet and don't panic, stay focused, the runs will come.

PS—Don't forget to practice on the good days to make sure you survive the bad ones.

Master your batting.

The crisis is here—even before there's a career!

Like much else, the age and stage at which a career crisis can hit you seem to come earlier and faster all the time.

The initial encounter with our first crisis in the workplace is usually the most challenging. The younger, less experienced worker tends to have a magnified view of whatever he/she feels is going wrong at the workplace. In contrast to the slightly older, hopefully wiser, semi-cynical professional who has by then hopefully acquired a this too shall pass approach to turbulent phases in flight, the first-time flyer, so to say, begins to visualise the plane crashing and his worst fears coming true with every air pocket. The personal sense of self-worth of a young worker is sometimes very strongly tied up with the first few years of proving himself outside the sheltered home existence of earlier years; so a designation change, a reprimand, a transfer, a demotion or, at worst, a sacking are all capable of causing massive, intense personal turmoil and an all is finished response. Mood swings and panic attacks are almost default. How many of my colleagues in the newspaper industry have actually had nightmares about pages going wrong to press is no joke.

When you read the daily papers, you realise that so often major road tragedies occur when a driver does something abruptly to avoid a relatively minor mishap and that error of judgement leads to an infinitely larger one. A bus that skids on an oil patch may end up hitting the road divider, but when the driver lunges at the steering to avert that impact, he sometimes takes the bus off the road altogether into a ravine, and a dozen passengers to their end with him. Far better to brace for the minor collision and handle minor repairs, in retrospect— but at that moment, the mind often doesn't work. Inexperienced drivers usually aggravate situations in which they are caught by panicking and losing control and that panic is what kills when the initial situation, if checked with a controlled mind, would at best have needed some broken lights replaced.

The panicky rookie's response to a work pressure situation is sometimes like that. The *crisis* is often a 5/10 in work difficulty terms, but the manner in which it is responded to, often, serves to blow it up into a full-fledged episode with the potential to derail both the psychological growth of the individual and the CV.

The perfectly natural response to an emerging career crisis—something that's never been encountered and leaves the individual flummoxed—is the immediate need to find advice and solace on how to handle it. That is, of course, a very good idea. What is not a very good idea is to have mummy/papa/jiju and whoever is there on the dining table chart out that course of action—with all due respect, they don't know how exactly you're placed. The second not-so-good idea is to sit down with a circle which agrees totally and completely and emotionally that it's you who is getting a 100 per cent raw deal and spurs your angst and anguish further, and tells you that they are with you. I don't mean to be mean—or maybe I do—but sometimes all offices can make out the Losers' Clubs from a distance. You know, the ones who don't have solutions for their own recurring professional issues—and you can make out that they don't—and find solace in knowing that none of them have it, which must mean that the system sucks and can't appreciate their genius.

Some time back, I encountered the case of a young worker, a new joinee, who had the basic skills and the background to have done very well, despite the initial flak she began drawing when she entered the system, primarily on account of small oversights, lack of attention to detail—nothing non-repairable. The problem was that instead of reflecting on why she was getting flak, she found her first line of emotional solace on the shoulders of others already in the line of flak. So instead of talking to the ones who rarely ever got shot and understanding how they did what they did, she got into the pattern of sharing the day's trauma over tissues and lunch with the others who had got immune to being shot, what I (very nastily) referred to as the Collective Losers' Club. That didn't help her at all. Great for catharsis, I guess, but what else?

And this wasn't just her. Gradually, you begin to find this flocking together, this accumulation of aggrieved souls who have decided that Life Here Sucks, pretty early in the work scene, and who then spend more time wiping each other's tears than in trying to ensure that they outgrow the daily cycle of bad work-flak-mutual therapy session.

So, I took a print of this from a piece by Fred Kofman and tacked it up:

> We all want to be liked, as Dave Kerpen writes. The problem is that rather than following Dave's counsel, many of us attempt to be liked through *Idiot Compassion*. We collude with the person stuck in the victim mindset. We blame, we moan and groan.
>
> 'I can't believe they did that to you!' 'They shouldn't have!' 'You deserve better than that.' 'They should fix it right now!'
>
> These comments are soothing – like a drug – and equally deadly. They calm you down with sweet protection and rev you up with righteous indignation. But they *don't* give you a way to address the situation. You may think the person making them is on your side, *but your drug dealer is not your friend.* (Chaturvedi, emphasis added)

If I thought this was too highbrow for a 22-year old, I was pleasantly surprised at how clearly and how immediately it made its way through. It's not that there have been no other hassles in the year or so since then—office would be so boring if we have none, right?—but the fact is that today, when she feels that she's the victim in a given situation, at least she knows that the drug dealer is not her friend. So we find other more lasting, less bitter models of agreeing to disagree. On the whole, from being someone lost when she was under pressure, she knows she can fight her battles back—by herself. That, to me, is a way bigger achievement than a three-rank promotion.

Another colleague sometimes has a divergent take from mine when I am arguing 'the drug dealer' point. If young people will not go to their immediate friends' circle to share and seek feedback and catharsis, she asks, 'Where will they go? Isn't it the most natural thing to do? Isn't that what they do in school and college? Aren't bosses and seniors often inaccessible and intimidating? Where is someone being shot by the boss at the workplace to go for solace—the boss who is shooting her or the friends who, inexperienced though they be, at least give her a shoulder to cry on?'

She has a point.

My counter argument is that by extension, picking up a cigarette when two of your friends smoke can also be the most natural thing to do—but your lungs will not necessarily appreciate that natural addition to your life, and that gesture of solidarity or bonding will cost you a lot personally in the long run. And if you can have the common sense to not pick up a cigarette even if your immediate friends' circle smokes, you can very well have the common sense to not pick up shared responses to work situations, no matter how well you bond as individuals. If five friends get married tomorrow, they will necessarily have to work out the individual equations of their respective personal lives by themselves; and it will be rare for one to have solutions for what issues another faces in his/her marriage. Career growth and career questions are as uniquely individual and can often be distorted by outsourcing decision making to a pool. Finally, we all have to work out our work basics in our own mind. Whether you want to do it via conversations with the tyrannical boss, or by observing the benevolent senior, or by chatting up colleagues who are clearly doing better at work in the long run, or by reading up on the topic—stuff like this book, perhaps—is a factor of what you're comfortable with. If the questions trouble you, the need to find your answers will push you to search for them and work your long-term fundamentals out. I often ask newcomers, 'What is your work philosophy?' It stumps many—but not as many as I would expect. You have to know why you've come to work, beyond the day's salary. You have to find, for want of a better parallel, where the North on your compass is. That way, at least, even if you make mistakes—and you will make mistakes—you learn from them directly. I found my personal compass in someone as unexpected as Vivekananda, and so the solutions of my initial crisis years—and beyond—came from him. That story of endless crisis management is summed up in a piece I wrote a couple of years back in The Speaking Tree, which I'm reproducing here, now. It may give you some sense of how I attempted to retain a degree of sanity when faced with situations beyond my comprehension abilities. It talks about when I started out an inconsequential career in the back of beyond and more.

I had to find my answers. You have to find yours.

My Teen Icon wore Saffron[2]

Long, long ago, I too—unlikely as it may seem with the greying hair today—was once a teen-aged rebel. Defiant, stubborn, questioning, a risk-taker, even reckless. Some of those traits I have, hopefully, retained. But the instigator of my transition from a seemingly inconspicuous docile schoolboy to this combative version was neither my college gang nor a rapper with an exotic name. It was a man long dead, having lived all of 39 years, speaking to me through fiery words that did not diminish in intensity with the passage of time.

I picked up Vivekananda's thoughts one day in class XII, and have not quite been able to put them down yet. Having the capability to live only a little of what he practised, I cannot lay claim to being Eklavya to his Dronacharya status. Yet, when I was beginning to decipher the questions of right and wrong, moral and immoral, he summed it up for me the complexity of it all: 'Fear is the greatest sin my religion teaches.' Since then, I've tried to ensure that I did not commit the cardinal sin, whatever other errors I make.

During childhood, I learnt, as we all do, that convention and what everyone else thought mattered. Then I unlearnt it. 'I will die a 1000 deaths rather than lead a jelly-fish existence and yield to every requirement of this foolish world,' the monk thundered through the years into my mind space, and is it any wonder that I was often more

of a nonconformist than anyone with a dozen tattoos, eyebrow piercings and purple hair colour
could have been?

When I was at my most despondent, wondering whom to turn to for help, unsure of receiving
it from anywhere, I recalled the man who wrote:

> Human help I spurn with my foot. He who has been
> with me through hills and dales, through deserts and
> forests, will be with me, I hope; if not, some heroic soul
> would arise some time or other, far abler than myself,
> and carry it out.

I learnt to not despair for human help and reconcile to the fact that either He would chart out
my survival or declare an end to my tenure here.

When I started out an inconsequential career
in the back of beyond, I sometimes wondered
what I was doing, whether it was all that I was
worth. Vivekananda told me—'Do not be afraid
of small beginnings, great things come after-
wards. Be courageous.' I learnt not to despair at
small beginnings and have the courage of great
things to follow them.

When I faced flak, I remembered the monk
writing to his boys: 'Have faith that you are all,
my brave lads, born to do great things! Let not
the barks of puppies frighten you—no, not even

the thunderbolts of heaven—but stand up and work!' He almost read my mind and explained in his fiery fashion: '[T]he names of those who will wish to injure us will be legion. But is not that the surest sign of our having the truth? The more I have been opposed, the more my energy has always found expression.' And I stood up and worked, irrespective of the disapproval of puppies and the heavens alike. And learnt to no longer cringe at those wishing to injure. And lived to tell the tale—so far!

When I faced slander and innuendo, my first reactions were hypersensitive. I itched to get even. Then I went back to the monk who was not spared, when in the USA, by critics questioning his way of life there. And his response: 'Tell my friends that a uniform silence is all my answer to my detractors. If I give them tit for tat, it would bring me down to a level with them. Tell them that truth will take care of itself...' I learnt to not respond and to believe that facts would take care of themselves.

When I wistfully looked at the 20s go by in 12-hour work days and struggle and little else, when I looked around and wondered why I had neither money nor fame and whether my nonconformity was worth anything, Vivekananda told me to wait. Wait, he said, 'Wait, money does not pay, nor name; fame does not pay, nor learning. It is love that pays; it is character that cleaves its way through adamantine walls of difficulties.' I looked back at the worst points of my life, saw for myself whether I lasted through them because I kept the backbone straight or because I had clout or cash, got my answer and told myself not to forget it thence.

When the instinct to do earth-shattering things egged me on, only to be killed with one look at my dismal bank balance, I asked him for answers, and he told me: 'Was it ever in the history of the world that any great work was done by the rich? It is the heart and the brain that do it ever and not the purse.' I stopped assuming that I was incapable of great work if my purse was empty.

It has now been many years of long hours and busy schedules and sometimes one wants to simply be quiet and put thoughts into words, but time is scarce in the pursuit of the daily bread. But then one recalls the monk, even in his situation in life, writing to Sister Nivedita: 'I was born for the life of a scholar—retired, quiet, poring over my books. But the mother dispenses otherwise—yet that tendency is there.' And for a moment my master and me are kindred spirits, joined in a thought across a century.

And as I chart the journey of what years I have lived and what years—who knows how many—are left, every single time I face something that makes me falter, ponder, slow down, I go back to my *gurumantra*, words of Vivekananda that are etched in my mind from that day when I first read them as a 17-year old: 'This I have seen in life—he who is overcautious about himself falls into dangers at every step; he who is afraid of losing honour and respect, gets only disgrace; he who is always afraid of loss, always loses...'

When Vivekananda taught that to a 17-year old, he gave him freedom from fear; he made him the ultimate teenaged rebel. Except that, unlike the tattoos, the piercings or the punk cuts, you never outgrow this rebel instinct.

You gifted me the ability to stay in my mind forever 17. Happy birthday, Naren!

Notes

1. First published in *The Times of India*. 2007. 'The Speaking Tree', 25 February.
2. First published in *The Times of India*. 2011. 'The Speaking Tree', 9 January.

PART III

6

Don't fragment your thinking. Learn to cut stuff out

Pythagoras wrote: 'Learn to be silent. Let your quiet mind listen and absorb.'

I was awful at Maths in school, and let it go at the first chance I got, and that line is pretty much the only thing I remember from anyone remotely connected with algebra or geometry or whatever. But I'm quite certain it has been infinitely more relevant to the business of my everyday life than whatever the ratios between the sides of some triangle are, could have ever been.

In the era of great emphasis on free speech, on the power of expression, on communication skills, on broadcasting what you are, how you are and living life as a 24/7 talk show, we've come to venerate speech so much that we're obsessed with it. We go *ooh* and *aah* over the inanest of things said, partly by political correctness, partly by bored reflex. Being asked to Shut Up or Keep Quiet is the same as being oppressed, victimised, insulted, sidelined. We have to make ourselves heard! We equate a vague sense of freedom or power with speech, and silence with irrelevance or oppression.

And that drains us of so much we could be, we could do.

The point is not that there is no silence in our life at all. Of course there is. Often, lots of it.

The point is that one has to, literally, *learn* to be silent.

Because the silence we need to spend time with is not the silence of fatigue. It is not the silence of depression and heartbreak and staring at photos of happier times and reading texts from your friends on how your ex is now so happy with his current GF. It is not the silence of sulking in a party because the person you came to it with is hitting on someone else or your BFF trashed what you wore to it. It is not the silence of sitting alone in your room from 11 pm to 4 am with just a few nasty comments which came your way in the day playing on loop to keep you company, the TV screen flickering with muted volume, wondering if the world doesn't get you, or is the problem finally somewhere within you, after all? It is not the silence of staring fixatedly at your toes or your nails or the carpet in a meeting, fervently hoping the boss won't turn to you for an idea and will continue to be distracted and not notice your existence. No, this is not *that* silence.

This silence is the silence of allowing your mind to settle. It is the silence of giving space to yourself to know what you are thinking, what you are feeling.

We are fined by the law from texting or taking calls—essentially, for doing things that *distract* us—while driving. We ought to fine ourselves for indulging in a 100 times more distractive, non-sensical, suicidal behaviour while driving our careers, our reputations, our lives.

Swami Vivekananda may not have foreseen a reporter stopping filing to respond to 'hi, 'sup?' popping up on Gtalk even as she tries to file a story to a deadline, or had to remind colleagues furiously texting away to one of their 591 friends in the middle of a reporting ideas meeting that they haven't had a coherent idea in three days, as I sometimes have to, but the results of that fragmented mind's functioning are all too obvious and stretch across all that we do.

There is, sometimes, simply too much talk. Too much sharing. Too much support, too much debate. Too much energy spent in moving absolutely nowhere. A daily catharsis which leaves you *feeling* better but having learnt nothing from the things that led to those feelings. Twitter and Facebook are great, but beyond a point, what is the sharing about? Your mind is sometimes so, *so* conditioned to looking out, talking, reacting, watching, listening, laughing, commenting, that if you sit quietly by yourself, your buddies congregate to ask if everything's all right. *Thinking* or wanting to be quiet is for old people, sad people, incorrigible introverts, and for when things have gone horribly wrong and you want to be left alone to mope.

Or is it?

Ramakrishna once spoke about a still mind being like a tranquil pool which can reflect the moon in all its grandeur, while the average person's mind is like a pool in constant churn—the water never gets to settle down enough to have a surface calm enough that'll reflect what's above.

But this is not about *dhyaan*, nirvana or navel-gazing. We're talking careers, not *moksha*. This is about the endless dissipation of energy in thousands and thousands of words typed out and exchanged which, while being very good indexes of our being social and friendly and sweet and popular and all that, leave us with time and energy that's barely enough for us to recharge, to absorb things and thoughts. And growth comes by absorbing, by listening. Not by reaching out 24/7. Not by reacting to what people say or do to us all the time.

The world will manage without our goodwill, too. What Ramakrishna said to Vivekananda in a different context applies just as much to us: *First Have Something To Give*. First build yourself. Find your own clarity of mind, before volunteering to become the principal emotional and professional advisor to people around you. How can I solve your Maths queries when my own scores in Maths left me cringing? How can I be presumptuous enough to advise you how to handle your boss if I've never been a boss myself for 48 hours?

I think we need to communicate less, not more. We need to have fewer people on our Facebook, and spend fewer hours of our life Liking the latest recycled quote they post and appreciating the very stock picture which they uploaded and which 66 people are gushing about. Being the 67th won't make you friends for life, ignoring it won't make you lifelong enemies. So don't provide evidence that you're bored, disinterested and unoccupied by consuming and generating inane conversation. Do something better with your time. Don't become someone who has to squeal his/her emotions out in 140 characters at every traffic signal, every office meeting, every meal consumed. All of us have to handle traffic and office and almost everything else you do. It's not really worth spending energy on.

Equations are great, and friendship is what defines youth in some ways, the gangs and the buddies and the circles—or they don't, depending on what degree of an extrovert or introvert you are. It's fine either way. All I'd suggest is—don't be overly obsessed with your social circle at the workplace. I have never once seen anyone quit in solidarity because their best friend was sacked. So you won't have that buddy walking next to you for the coffee or the lunch or whatever the day she gets a different job, or the boss has had enough of her. Make friends, yes, but don't make friends at the cost of personal bonding taking priority over work *at the work-place*. Spend all your off days and your vacations and move in with your buddy if you want—but remember, *when you work*, you can't make it an extension of your personal and emotional equations. Relationships break off. Reputations live on. Someday, your personal skills and reputation will be your strongest assets. Don't undersell it for your current boyfriend or your office mamma or your soul sister.

In a phase where I was even meaner than I am currently as a boss, after failing to get the point across about relentless chatter impacting work adversely and consistently, I put up a large poster in the office bay with these lines by Alexander Pope in an attempt to embarrass the chatterati. It didn't work. But anyway, this is what he said:

Words are like leaves
And where they most abound
Much fruit of sense beneath
Is rarely found

We are losing the basics of concentrated work. When I was studying for my class XII Boards, not that I did anything fabulous finally, I tacked up a quote by Henry Ward Beecher which I've carried around since then: 'One intense hour will do more than dreamy years.'

No, I don't always manage to live by it. I wish I could, though.

I've wasted dreamy years doing little, but the point remains fundamentally true. It is so much easier to have a dreamy day drift by than to occupy our mind for one intense hour. We are so used to the fragmented mind model, we are so proud of eternally multitasking, that the very concept of concentrated mental effort, leaving all else aside, is now an alien one, something which nerds and crazy scientists are supposed to do. We—including me—text while driving, check phones while conversing, respond to mails while writing, chat around while working.

We have given away the power to interrupt our mental flow of thought to anyone who chooses to walk up to us, to call us, to send us an email, an SMS, a BBM, a WhatsApp. The world walks into our mind without knocking 18 hours a day. We are too defensive about not responding since then we expect to be tagged as snooty or 'too busy' or insensitive or uncaring or, god forbid, 'having changed.' Then, we are transfixed before the TV. What's going on? So much of this means nothing more than the 'How're you?' exchanges at parties—both sides have usually moved on before the other has responded. You say stuff for the sake of saying it. It means zilch. Cut it out. Downsize your social circle. Declutter your conversations. Declutter your timelines. Declutter your *mind* so you can reach out and find what you need when you need it. Don't, *don't* keep it like a muddled trashy worktable. It's pretty much your most relevant professional degree.

The power of concentrated thought is so, so, so hugely underrated, it's not funny. Most of us are taking nine hours to do what we could have finished in five. We have less free time in hand because we drift through so much of our day— yes, we are working, nobody's denying that, but effective work is not necessarily *efficient* work. In the profession that I have worked in so far, the difference in how someone writes a story amidst chats and conversations and pings, and how someone writes it in one clear, coherent go, is so, so vast that it nullifies a five-year advantage of experience which a fragmented mind would otherwise have had over an inexperienced but focused one. Too many of us, in our 20s, 30s or even 40s, are like schoolchildren who sit on the playground bench and can't help swinging their feet—we're too restless, almost habituated to focusing only *under pressure*—and then, too, half the focus is on how much the pressure is.

I hardly have the second—or for that matter the thousandth—most important job in the country. I'm middle-class, middle-aged, middle-management. But I also have to learn to shut off time zones. I have to learn to keep the phone aside if I have to speak to someone. I have to let go of the mail-checking impulse for a couple of hours if I am inflicting an insufferably boring meeting on those poor souls paying for karmic oversights of previous births. I *have* to put the odd DND tag on my cabin if I am writing something that needs uninterrupted thought. You can't live life as an open-door policy, have things tossed into your thought space at random 24/7, *and* take your thinking to anything beyond its existing level, any more than you can look to build SRK's *Om Shanti Om* six-packs in your 40s while gobbling down every plate of *samosa* and *gulabjamun* extended your way in the wedding season.

My kids in school are taught (not that they follow it): Say No To Junk Food.

I try to Say No To Junk Communication. I can't afford to be out of shape, mentally. Neither can you.

If you read your Amar Chitra Kathas carefully, you have a rough idea of what all those *rishi*s with matted locks were doing before they emerged and turned people into stones or cursed generations or whatever, don't you? Most of them were not acclaimed public speakers—they tended to, like hibernating bears, be tucked inside caves for endless stretches of time. Alone. Quiet. The basic rationale of enhancing what your mind can do by occasionally—or frequently—voluntarily embracing solitude is not a new one. No, I don't want to curse anyone. But my abilities to understand, to grasp, to empathise, to react—they are all heightened when I have invested in quiet time, in solitude.

I was intrigued when I read S. Radhakrishnan use the word 'duty' in this context. One of the lines messily underlined in my ragged copy of his commentary on the Bhagvad Gita is part of his comment on VI:10. He says: 'In a world which is daily growing noisier, the duty of the civilised man is to have moments of thoughtful stillness.'

You've of course seen the Keep Calm And Carry On posters, and their derivatives. I'd like one plastered all around which says, Keep Quiet And Finish Kaam. Silence and single-minded focus tend to go well together, or so I think. One who cannot practice the former will often find it difficult to achieve the latter, though worthier— or more exceptional—minds than yours or mine may perhaps manage it.

So what's the crux? Focus, focus, focus. *Meditation* isn't jazz—it could get you the boss's cabin, or, failing which, render you immune to the bullets flying from the boss's cabin. Either way, life's chilled.

Oh, and I haven't brought in the Vivekananda quote here yet, I realise. He has this base covered, too, in a way: 'When you are doing any work, do not think of anything beyond. Do it… as the highest worship, and devote your whole life to it for the time being.'

I'm not suggesting that you have to embrace a monastic lifestyle or basics for this to apply to your career. I'm just proposing that when we drift through work zones with so much other stuff occupying our mind, we are behaving like the motorcyclists who have blaring music plugged into their ears even as they attempt to cross an unmanned railway crossing, oblivious to the train heading their way.

The results aren't pretty.

7

Don't overrate the praise. Don't overreact to the sniping

I began to be told, see, now you've established yourself as an actor, now you need to be doing what the typical Hindi film heroine has to do—the song and dance routines. The glam quotient. My heart is not in that; it doesn't come naturally to me. So I started making an effort and I didn't realise that everyone couldn't know everything. But those are things you only learn with experience. I began to try to adapt to the mould of the typical Hindi film heroine. And I was making a fool of myself. *Thappad pad raha tha mujhe* and rightfully so. *Har jagah se.* And at that time, you begin to develop a sense of victimisation, the whole world is out to get you.

It reached a stage where random people would walk up to me and say things. I was getting my manicure and this lady comes up to me and asks, 'You're so pretty, why do you wear such bad clothes?' And I used to be like, 'Who's given you the right to talk to me like that?' People would say I shouldn't step out of the house because of the sort of clothes I wore. And I would take all of it seriously. I think at that time my confidence had again dipped to a 3. Today, I'm back at a 10!

That's Vidya Balan, in an interview to *Delhi Times*, which, incidentally, I took, in July 2013, shortly after *Dirty Picture* had catapulted her into the national limelight. Here, she was talking about the years where her choice of films and her choice of clothes and her choice of pretty much everything were drawing flak.

If you notice, she begins this by talking about 'I began to be told...' and towards the end reiterates, '...I would take all of it seriously.' And tells you that the phase in which she was paying the most attention to what she was being told was also the phase where her confidence was a 3/10.

What am I trying to say here?

It's very simple. You can't keep everyone happy—so don't try to and don't overreact to peer feedback, good or bad. Don't let what other people around you say start shaping the direction you head in; that's the surest guarantee of being directionless.

As you begin to come to grips with the initial years of your career, you will inevitably experience a lot of confusion, have a lot of questions, engage in a lot of conversation, ask for a lot of advice and get doled out a lot of unsolicited opinion along the way. While it is common sense to listen to people as you attempt to comprehend the professional and social dynamics of wherever you work, it is equally important to *not* listen to a lot of stuff from a lot of people and to be careful about whose advice you actually put into practice. There is no deficiency of quack advice floating about in almost every office—and it's you who will pay for listening to it, not the dispenser of *gyaan*. This is like being offered a smoke as a solution to stress; it looks like the person giving it is being friendly and helpful, whereas actually he's setting you up to die prematurely. And painfully.

Second, apart from such *gyaan*—which is, at least on the face of it, nice stuff which can later actually harm you—you will also have to, at some point or the other, face less welcome stuff which can be described in many different ways, depending on the nuances: Flak; Criticism; Gossip; Slander; Bullying; Bitching;

Character Assassination, etc. You will initially think that such stuff doesn't (or can't) happen to you because you keep to yourself, you're not really the gossiping kinds, you just do your work and close for the day. Now, this may be true. And yet, it will make very little difference. The amount of attention the resident goss experts give to you is often completely unconnected to what you do or not do. Often, *not* being part of chat circles invites even greater chat about you since the group of the underworked five who have sat down for a leisurely goss session obviously can't goss about each other—at least not while they all are there—so the one who is not likely to ever be buddies with any of them is the easiest to dig their claws into, guilt free. Anyone who gets to hear of stuff said behind his/her back and asks, 'But what's their *problem*?' is just being naive. You can't address their problem. What you can do, however, is not let it become yours.

While there cannot be a textbook response to how to go about this, I would suggest a few rules of thumb to not go under or get frazzled and hassled by the absolutely inevitable occurrence of the *why did she say that?* phenomenon.

- *Don't* let casual, nasty, bitchy, snide comments change your primary reflexes, demotivate or derail you. Comments are for free. Sniping is as much part of the workplace as sledging is part of cricket. Learn to ignore it if you can. If you can't ignore it, learn to handle it without losing your cool or your confidence. Don't react to things the way drivers react at the slightest touch of another car's bumper—by pulling up instantly and creating a scene on the road. The Australians have perfected the art of making comments about the batsmen at the crease to break their concentration, and it works very well for them. A Dravid or a Laxman or a Sachin has however rarely been tripped by that, and usually preferred to respond by showing them the scoreboard rather than the middle finger, and that's what differentiates the men from the forever-adolescent boys in a sense. The Sreesanth model of launching into a war dance in response to any provocation is not really a sustainable one. Just the way you'll be teased for the things you get irked by in primary school, you'll be sniped at more if you engage in running battles. Ignore, avoid, disengage. Don't abuse those who snipe at you. They don't have loving you as part of their job contract, and they don't need to. If you still want to get even with them, work better than them, become their boss.

- *Don't* let those friends or well-wishers who have no stake in the outcome instigate and egg you on to stupid or angst-filled reactions. Even if they aren't like bystanders egging on a drunkard in a pub brawl just for the fun of it (which is often the case), and they *actually* mean you well, they'll in all likelihood still end up doing you no good. Learn to ignore your friends the way you do your enemies sometimes. Do not be the chronic hysteria-filled person who incessantly rants to his/her advisory circle, and then is pumped up by them for retaliatory action. There is nothing more juvenile. I have seen far too many cases, regrettably, of people who were initially perfectly fine when reprimanded for making a mistake, realising what they had done—and then, post a counselling session with friends, had woken up to how that reprimand was in fact a grave injustice to them and a breach of all global rules of fair play. That's just being daft and telling everyone that you don't know what you think till someone else tells you. That's just sad. Don't, *don't* play to the gallery. Don't be egged on to taking up fights by anyone else. There are no collective calls in careers. Even today, I have to check myself from reacting on the rare occasions when I take an unexpectedly conciliatory tone on a work issue and promptly get a passing remark from my team about how I have *gone all soft* these days. Maybe I have. But I have to check my responses— I can't go around tearing into other departments simply to retain the swashbuckling image in my own. Whatever the image is, will be a factor of how I work, and that's fine. It can't be the other way round. This isn't college.

- *Don't* overreact to the supposedly concerned-about-you resident gossiper when he/she brings you the latest goss about who did what or who said what about you. If at all you must listen, store it, but don't act on it, don't form quick judgments based on hearsay. Discount the veracity of all gossip by 50 per cent as a default setting and then see if it is still worth your response. Do not develop animosity for a colleague under the influence of someone else's reporting—go by your own impressions and common sense. Chinese whispers are played out many times over in office grapevines, and what you finally get to hear may be a very distorted version of what originally happens. Have a few people you know and trust, who do not enjoy or live off spicy half-truths. Seek their viewpoint on how accurate something can be, if it really bothers you. Don't let it stew in your head. All other things apart, it's physically and emotionally draining. Many years back, the first time I got to hear *goss* about me, in vivid detail, I couldn't focus for a week. Now, older and marginally wiser, I ask, 'Is that all? I must clearly be losing my relevance; I no longer attract the spiciest goss on the floor!'

Even if you're not exactly Miss Congeniality, that's no reason to get hassled or question your basic reflexes. The underlying beauty of the workplace's requirements is that 80 per cent of the time, even the Devil gets his/her due when he/she delivers what he/she has to, all else be damned. Too many people put up with even those quirks of the social system they are in which they don't really like, assuming that it's rude or damaging to keep their distance. 'I don't know why everyone comes and takes half an hour of my time to tell me about their life's woes. I want to tell them to go away and let me work, but I can't', a young colleague complained recently, attributing it to her sympathetic looks and nodding at appropriate points whenever such a narration came her way. I had to explain that finally, the work that she didn't do on account of this free counselling would get her shot, and so it would simply amount to her shortly going around with *her* tale of woes to those people.

Beyond a point, the bedrock of your job is your skill, your expertise, your ability to deliver good results consistently. The social dynamics of only *those* cricketers are discussed who are able to stay in the team by going out on the ground and scoring runs and taking wickets and gobbling up the catches that come their way. If you are consistently being clean bowled for 12 runs, being hit for 25 in an over and spilling straightforward catches which are then replayed in slow motion making you look like a complete idiot over and over, what your social dynamics with other players in the dressing room are won't interest anyone soon because you won't be *in* the dressing room, you'll be out of the team and watching the match on TV from your living room. Do Virat and Dhoni get along is something that merits goss, assuming that both are an integral part of the team? As of today, nobody discusses whether Dhoni and Sehwag get along. And why is that? Because Sehwag isn't in the team from months—because he doesn't score runs anymore. So, *now* who gives a damn about whether they get along or not? If he single-mindedly was obsessed with his batting and could keep his batting average going, the intra-team people dynamics would be incidental. Once he's not a master of his primary skill, hitting the leather ball with the willow, he's not even relevant enough for who loves and who hates him to matter.

Remember that: who loves and who hates you will be talked about *till the point you deliver on your job.*

The easiest way to not be talked about at all is to fail at work. You'll be irrelevant, and the gossipers will move on to more engaging topics. Would Monica Lewinsky have gained global headlines if she was, err, fraternising with a cabbie? But the Prez *matters*—and he's more goss friendly. The whole paparazzi phenomenon works on the basic premise that people like to consume gossip about high-profile, successful individuals. But to be successful in the first place, they didn't need the media—they needed to work, and work well, for long periods of time. The flashbulbs often blind us to that.

This is how I see it:

- *Efficient, Competent + Social, Congenial =* Are you for real?! They'll probably never let you go
- *Efficient, Competent + Unsocial, Reserved* = You'll do just fine. Don't worry. You came here for respect, not hugs, right?
- *Inefficient, Incompetent + Social, Congenial* = Short-term survival. PR skills take you only so far. You'll go from support to sympathy to indifference to exit pretty quickly—it's a question of when, not if
- *Inefficient, Incompetent + Unsocial, Whiny* = Why don't you just quit today and spare everyone the torture, really?

The solution to not ending up in the latter two categories is to take out time, serious time, to decide what you're here for, what you want to do, what you want to become—and then feed in that destination in your GPS, so to say. Else, you'll be like a driver who's new to a place and is seeking directions from everyone hitching a ride in the car—they may all have different takes and at the end of the day, if you haven't found the location you came for, it's still fundamentally your fault. A compass needs space around it to be able to find its true north. Having a dozen opinionated friends, enemies and frenemies shape how you go about things is pretty much the same as placing a compass in the middle of half a dozen magnets and shuffling them around—it'll just keep swivelling from one direction to the other, and you can keep doing that for hours without getting any sense of direction, literally.

Your career is infinitely more important than your figure, right? OK, it's *almost* as important. The point is that your diet or exercise regimes are finally about what works for *you*. If you were to change them depending on how someone says you're looking on a given day, or use flattering or unflattering remarks to decide what you'll do the next day, you'll have no consistency of plan or action, and after a year you may well have 52 different weekly plans executed which finally didn't lead you very far— while one plan which you stuck to for 52 weeks with bull-headed tenacity would at least show you clearly whether it worked for you or not, either way.

And if you think commentary, opinion, sniping, dissection are a temporary phase, and you can get away with not really working out a solution to it in your head, you're dead wrong. This isn't something that will fade out with time or seniority—it's not acne. In fact, once you become a team leader or a boss, it will only amplify, and if you get to be the boss based on your skills but by that time haven't worked out your responses to all this, you'll collapse because it'll come at you with double or triple the intensity that you currently have to deal with at the not-so-senior levels. I have this quote by Perry M. Smith on my table for the past 7–8 years to remind me that:

Russian military philosophy on leadership emphasises the important point that *the higher the post you occupy, the more strictly you will be judged.* A leader is *bound* to be criticised, both fairly and unfairly, by associates within the organisation, by bosses and their staff, and by competitive organisations and individuals. A leader who therefore becomes thin-skinned when criticised, or who becomes defensive, is doing a disservice to the organisation.[1] (Chaturvedi, emphasis added)

Robin Sharma makes much the same point when he says:

> Leadership is not a popularity game. It's not about doing what's easy. It's about doing what's right. We are too bothered about being judged. Or about what people are thinking. We *will* be judged. People *will* talk about us. So be it. Move on, work.[2]

I was being dissed when I was 25; I'm being decoded when I am 41. It never went away, it only changed form or—more often—escalated. Some things remained constant (such as 'What *does* he think of himself?!'), others changed with roles and tasks. It helped greatly that by 27 or thereabouts I had learnt to respond with a blank, expressionless face when someone walked up to me and said something like 'you must have been really lucky to have been given this role at this age; did they know your family?' or 'you poor chap, they're giving you *that* department? Why did you agree, it's going to be the end of your career!' Incidentally, I was given both these pearls of wisdom by two senior colleagues on the same day. It helped me gain clarity that everyone had their two-penny worth on what was going on in my life, much of it contradictory, so I let it neutralise itself out and opted to thereafter pretend that I was paying attention and forget all about what they said as soon as they were done with imparting that day's quota of sympathy or praise. At that point, I also began to understand Vivekananda's perspective when, doing infinitely more flamboyant work than mine, he wrote, 'Let the world say what it chooses, I shall tread the path of duty... Otherwise, if one has to attend day and night to what this man says or that man writes, no great work is achieved in this world.'

Much later, when I was for a period caught in almost incessant battling and flak, I found what Lincoln—a man who faced more hatred and abuse in his presidency than most men would ever need to do in a lifetime—felt about those who opted to run him down and put that up on my already overcrowded office tack board:

> If I tried to read, much less answer, all the criticisms made of me, and all the attacks leveled against me, this office would have to be closed for all other business. I do the best I know how, the very best I can. And I mean to keep on doing this, down to the very end. If the end brings me out all wrong, ten angels swearing I had been right would make no difference. If the end brings me out all right, then what is said against me now will not amount to anything.

Anyway, we began this with Vidya Balan. It makes sense to end with her, too. Vidya has come out of a struggling 20s to an absolutely rocking 30s. It *may* be a coincidence that she has also come out from being oversensitive to feedback in her 20s to becoming a totally I-don't-give-a-damn-if-you-are-shocked individual who is having fun in her 30s—but I don't think it is fun, I think it is cause and effect. See what she said in that interview. Cut out the *as an actor* and substitute it with *as a young worker*, and see if it doesn't make sense to you.

> Today, when I look back, I realise that as an actor, you amplify everything. When the perceptions of people about you are larger than life, you begin to take their appreciation and their criticism also as larger than life. I had begun to amplify all that. I had begun to tell myself that *ab toh karna hi hai*, I have to prove to everyone that I can also do the other end of the spectrum. But I failed miserably. I got slapped around. *The reason why clothes and my weight and my choice of films came under such criticism was because I was doing so much of it to prove a point.* Maybe I was trying desperately to be what I was not, doing things that I was not enjoying doing.
>
> And I got slapped around so much that I went through a long period of deliberations and conversations with my family, with my close friends. And I summed up that I'm unhappy, and the whole world is unhappy with

me. So let me at least make myself happy; I'll probably never be able to have the world happy with me. And the moment I did that, accepting myself, I started becoming acceptable to everyone else.

It worked for her. I think it works for us. Don't prove any point, don't amplify the appreciation and criticism that comes your way. Relax, give up futile please-all endeavours, and find your own True North. Once you become acceptable to yourself, you'll be surprised at how acceptable you become to everyone else.

Notes

1. Smith, Perry M. (1998). *How to Run an Organization Successfully: Rules & Tools for Leaders—A Down-to-Earth Guide to Effective Managing.* New York: Avery Publishing Group.
2. See http://waythingswork.blogspot.in/2008/03/leadership-seminar-of-robin-sharma.html. Retrieved on 11 September 2014.

8

Don't attribute to malice what can be explained by insecurity

So I typed in *how to handle an obnoxious co-worker* on Google. It took 0.35 seconds to give me about 4,77,000 results. Clearly, a lot of thought and energy is being spent on this topic.

But I am not trying to do a dissection of the types of people who get your goat at work—from the clueless intern attached to you—despite your protestations—who doesn't seem to understand what you've told her three times already to the boss, who, well, ditto.

That's what office is about. Stuff will happen and people will be irrational, and so often people will not listen to you and so often you will listen with a jaw-dropping expression to something and then—unless you outrank them and there-fore can skewer them right back for their temer-ity—go back and say to yourself or to your office soulmate, 'What the hell is *wrong* with these people?'

At the end of the week or the month or the year, so much of our time is spent not on what we can do better, but on what other people are doing—either just out of curiosity (where does she find the time to put all that pancake on her face and still reach on time? I don't even get time to shampoo!!), or out of their figuratively poking us along the way (that lecture from nowhere I got from Voldemort in the morning—I'm pretty sure he was the one who ratted on me. What is the SOB's problem?).

Columnists and agony aunts tell us not to carry work back home. They have no clue. Who carries work back home? We carry the people from office back home. We love them, loathe them, dissect them, discover them, rediscover them, realise that we can't live without them, realise that we're without them and still living and generally have them in our iCloud of sorts, always there. They have more power to shape our office life, our choice to stay or leave, to do our best or to slink along, to want to come to work or to cry every morning before leaving, than anything which the company's CEO can do. A 30 per cent fall in our social equity has ramifications way, way beyond a 15 per cent change in our CTC when it comes to wanting or not wanting to do stuff, to stay on, to having that tranquil expression or the god-get-me-out-of-here-please look evident to all.

A disclaimer: This is not about taking home your office crush. A recent survey mailed out to the media said that some 29 per cent of workers have dated a co-worker, and that one in five office workers admits to having an office crush right now. Which means that, theoretically, every fifth person reading this has one. I'm not venturing into the domain of office romance or marrying someone on your floor. That's a different track altogether—and the dynamics of that are beyond the scope of this chapter, which deals with far more mundane stuff, not with finding the light of your life in the neon-lit corridors of the workplace.

My area of observation is how the irritation, the angst, the gradual I-don't-like-this-about-her/him seeps into our bloodstream a bit at a time. The bonding and the respect take time to come up, but the prejudices crop in quicker. We find a lot to laugh about in people and much less to learn from them.

Which is fine. A workplace is not a monastic order where you expect to absorb *gyaan* vibes all around. You will have idiots and jerks and losers and gossips and flirts and bosses' favourites who get away with half the work the rest do ostensibly just by fluttering their eyelashes, and that's a pretty good enough reason to hate them. Why should we not?

My impractical suggestion is for the *others* we don't like. The ones who are not really certified idiots and lechs and manipulators but we just don't like them anyway, for any number of reasons—for their mannerisms, their accents, their cocky dress sense, their wimpiness, their clinginess, their in-your-face-ness, their tendency to read our mails over our shoulders, their totally unwelcome comments on our work or our wardrobe, their frostiness towards us for no apparent reason—whatever. The point is, we don't really *hate* them—we just don't *like* them. And then we keep our distance.

Many years back, I was caught in a professional dilemma. We were in the week of sending the final appraisal forms for our team. One of my colleagues was about to be hitched to another person in the same company—not in my team—and that person was having troubles with his boss. There was some talk of a transfer. This colleague of mine was under a lot of pressure, and somehow the version of things that got around to her included that the boss of her special someone and I had basically colluded to get both of them posted out to simplify our lives and de-politicise the office atmosphere.

She barged into my room and without giving me a chance to speak, *tore* into me. About how I was sabotaging her career and her life, and how in order to keep my equation with the other big guns in office intact, I was willing to let junior careers be messed up and sacrificed so all of us in our cushy cabins could work out mutually convenient deals on things. She was half hysterical, half in tears, and I did not get much space to intervene and put across what had actually happened. The reality was that I hadn't as much as broached the issue anywhere, and the one option I had in mind at that point was to offer her a transfer from my side as well to the city her fiancé was going to be sent to, so maybe it would be easier for her.

I took all those insults without responding. Then she slammed the door and walked out. At first, I was mightily irked. What I wanted to type out was, 'If I really wanted to sabotage your career, I'd do a better job of it, trust me!' Of course, that was cheap, but I came close to sending it. The timing of that rant was classic because that evening was when I was filling in her annual appraisal. And I was so, so, so irked. I put aside her papers and left them for the next morning.

The point was not what sort of monetary increment or whatever would come her way from what I filled. The point was my ability to keep my objectivity while I filled it. I was just about 30 then, not really young enough to justify foolishness, yet not quite wise enough to have filled appraisals for a decade and have acquired a slightly more impartial tone to the annual conflict zone. I did not have a reference zone. I so wanted to bury that rating deep into the ground—to send the message that you mess with me this way at your expense; you don't insult me to my face and then strut out a star.

But the simple fact was that she had worked bloody hard the year round. She had done what she was entrusted to do. Whether that involved being Miss Congeniality was not the point. It was going to be an extremely personalised—and unjust—decision to nix her following that spat.

I spent two hours strolling on my terrace that night. It was complex. I had conflicting emotions, both fairly strong. It wasn't about her anymore. It was about me.

And my reference thoughts weren't about the Buddha and compassion. Or, as I sometimes tease juniors today, about Krishna and Shishupala, of the number of times one can overlook some line having been crossed. Or, about being the bigger person. I don't want to be the bigger person, heck, no. It's too taxing.

What I was going back to, was Perry M. Smith's very uncomplicated work advice to leaders: 'Wise leaders rarely attribute to malice that which can be adequately explained by stupidity.'[1]

In my mind, I was replacing *stupidity* with many other words. Insecurity. Unhappiness. Loneliness. Frustration. Irrational—or Justifiable—Anger. Persecution. Finally, it wasn't about arrogance, was it? It wasn't a diva telling me she was above the system and I could go to hell. It was about despair and frustration and a sense of the immediate universe conspiring against her—and I formed a key part of it.

In the morning, when I finally sent out the forms, I typed out a recommendation for a promotion for her.

In an odd sort of way, it was both of us being appraised—and I think that was the fairest thing to do. Which is not to say I haven't been unfair—I must be unfair a 100 times a year depending on who is on the other side—but had I let my pettiness and my two-penny bit of clerical power get the better of me that day, I think it would have rankled till today. Beyond that point—it is that person's destiny. That one rank would not have made or unmade her life anyway. If she was fab, she would grow no matter how much I attempted to cut her down; if she was flawed, she would stop soon no matter how much I patronised her. The point, therefore, was not about giving her a fair deal as some sort of charity. The point was—can I learn to not attribute to malice (and so, not respond with equal or greater malice) when things can be adequately explained by sentiments, by lonesomeness, by domestic situations, by illness, by sheer idiocy, by the 100 pressures the initial years of a career bring on a young person as they come to terms with how good they are—or they are not? As their dreams emerge and crash, as expectations rise and shatter, can we have, if not compassion, just a slightly higher degree of tolerance for those around us, sometimes, and let go their not-best-behaviour phases and try to not let that prejudice us?

One particular trait which I've seen over a decade—it may or may not hold true for all workplaces—is that often, skill and mastery of the craft come with a diminishing ability for compassion. Something akin to ragging of the next batch by those who are now the seniors. Of course, the workplace demands straight talk, no-nonsense feedback and sorted heads working in disciplined work systems; else, most of us won't have jobs tomorrow. I'm not saying people should not be shot for bad work.

What I'm saying is that those who enter the elite, unquestioned circles need to watch out that they don't mock while they mentor, don't forget the insecurities they themselves came through before being established, don't stand in a group and giggle at an error by a junior—a sort of error they probably made not many years back themselves. Flak hits people, but they can take it, often. Mockery hurts them, and those divides then are harder to bridge—so the workplace gradually divides itself into distinct social groups. Kill the bad worker—but kill him/her fair and square. Don't squeal with delight at his/her incompetence and then fall conspiratorially silent as she passes by, only to resume a nanosecond later. Those bridges are going to be irrevocably burnt. Grow out of that. Leave it in school. You may have to run your own team tomorrow. If that reflex stays with you, you'll find it tough to earn cooperation, forget about respect.

A lot of the best work in workplaces is done by the mavericks—the ones who think differently, have a slightly offbeat take on things, are not necessarily agreeing with the collective position. The way we collectively respond to them can either shut them up totally or give them the courage to at least speak up. There is no quicker way to stop someone from suggesting newer things than to face a collective uproar of laughter from a peer group when you're 10 days old and have an idea which you've in any case warily prefixed with 'I know this may sound stupid, but…' *Let* it sound stupid. Ideas from all possible ranks in systems can—and do—sound stupid; it is hardly the exclusive jurisdiction of the trainee or the new joinee alone. Stupid is also subjective. We are often too harsh on the initial blunders of the *outsider*. Yes, we're a rather unkind nation, we let people die on the road while we drive past; so this is hardly the apex of the tendency. But I'm making a very small point—though I confess I find it hard to follow myself.

Can we be a little kinder, a little more forgiving? Not let the daily interface with various sorts of human specimens diminish us as people? Let's just look at them as we watch unusual creatures at the zoo, perhaps, say, 'Wow, man, what way is that to do things?' and leave it at that. We don't get irked at chimpanzees or giraffes, do we? They're, well, different, they sure aren't like us, and we don't have to marry them. They can amuse us, bemuse us—but do we need to give them the right to irk us? Or to make us pettier, by making us into chronic, habitual analysts of their quirks? If you could see how many edgy and hyper-reactive people around at work are that way precisely because they don't have a sense of stability and belonging yet, you wouldn't grudge them much—more likely, walk up and tell them, hey, it's ok, if we were all out to get you, you probably wouldn't be here in the first place, right?

The well-known Internet quote says, 'Great minds discuss ideas; average minds discuss events; small minds discuss people.' Companies would prefer that we spend all the time after we punch in our card on solely discussing ideas. That's not going to happen. There is going to be a lot of discussion about people and events. That's inevitable. But perhaps, unless we know the whole story, we could be just a little kinder when we discuss them? That's possible, right?

Vivekananda, as you'd have noticed by now, makes one guest appearance in each chapter the way Subhash Ghai would in his movies. Again, when he discussed work, he was mostly addressing monks running monastic missions, but even in that spiritualised zone, he saw enough to write to his teams, so to say: 'We are all apt to think too highly of ourselves. We determine what our duties are to a much larger extent than we are willing to admit. Competition arouses envy, and kills the kindliness of the heart.'

And he does have it pretty much spot-on, in as few words as possible. Competition is inherent to work—it must be. What it sometimes does to us as people is the tougher part—it actually kills a lot of stuff within us. We become victorious in some battles at the cost of, as a colleague poetically once told me, 'No longer being the person I was.' In that case, it was a losing professional battle, not a victorious one, so technically it doesn't apply here, but I quote it nevertheless to make the point that we can go back as changed people—for better or worse—depending on the skirmishes, the angst, the sustained wish to tack people up and poke pins into their voodoo dolls or to run away from them altogether.

I'm just not sure if either the victories or the catharsis are worth it if they diminish *you* at the end of the day.

We spend so much time laughing at annoying co-workers sometimes that we overlook that we could be quite as annoying, if not more, to our colleagues. If we are the 'hostel seniors', in a sense, then it can be more than just annoying. I'm quite accustomed to the phenomenon, but many perfectly nice and sweet people would be astonished to know that someone went home and cried because of them! And yet it happens more often than you would guess.

This is not a compassion chapter. It's a self-reality check note, that's all. And that applies to you if you're 25, and it applies to me if I've done some 15 years after 25 making humongous mistakes, being mean, taking bad calls, snapping at people. I will get it wrong—but I have to know that I get it wrong, often. To help me not let my very average career give me a sense of exaggerated wisdom, I have put

up these very common-sense, non-philosoph-
ical lines from Perry M. Smith's book on my
tackboard:

> 'Do it all' leaders burn themselves out.
> 'Delegate it all' leaders lose touch.
> 'Sliders' postpone too many decisions.
> 'Hyper ambitious' leaders spend too much time impress-
> ing their bosses and depressing their followers.
> Wise leaders avoid these pitfalls through systematic
> introspection.[2]

I know that I will at some point or the other
meander towards one or the other of these oversights. There is no perfect wheel alignment on the
career road, at least in terms of our behaviour.
When I know I've messed up a week for my team,
I try to go back to the shortlist and see which
phase I was in—usually, given how many barbs I
get about 'when will you revert to my mail?' it's the
Slider. The pitfalls are kind of inevitable; the intro-
spection is optional—whether you're 42 or 22. And
so, at least once in a while, one attempts to keep
the wheels aligned and as they ought to be, or at
least keep oneself aware of which way the car's
tending to veer to because of the misaligned mind.

And that's how it is for many of us. We veer
here and there, we are upset, we are moody,

we are elated, we find a few moments of fab-ness and then often *it sucks* kicks right back in to fill the vacuum. Many of us perhaps have settled at the prospect of a non-depressing workplace and manage to get along with that as the benchmark—*happy* is a very big word to use. Someone—the boss, the boss's clique, the lobby, the nasty co-cubicle sharer, the ang-sty one who hates the visibility you are getting and makes it quite evident—someone or the other will give you reason to take a deep breath and either type out long messages to the BFF about what the F*** is their problem, or solve it with an extended weep session in the office washroom when the issue can't be held in long enough.

That's OK. You have no idea—even *they* may as of now be having an extended weep session, no matter how much jazzier their FB wall is. Take a deep breath. Nobody's done really enough yet for us to hate them that much. Later, maybe. Not now. It's too early to call the score. It's too early to let all that shape us. Our destinies aren't shaped by cubicle allotments or appraisal forms, and that's the simple truth of the matter. Let's get us sorted in our own heads—and then the other people as reference points will matter less and less for good or for bad.

I don't mean to bring philosophy here end-lessly, but sometimes—just sometimes—before launching into ripping into someone who per-haps quite deserved being ripped into—I've looked up to read from Max Ehrmann's *A Prayer* tacked above my table, the line *Spare me from Bitterness/and from the sharp passions of Unguarded Moments.*

And let it be.

I've never, yet, regretted sparing myself those Unguarded Moments.

Notes

1. Smith, Perry M. (1998). *How to Run an Organization Successfully: Rules & Tools for Leaders—A Down-to-Earth Guide to Effective Managing.* New York: Avery Publishing Group.
2. Ibid.

9

How you work is far, far more important than *what* work you do

I have a confession to make here.

This is *not* what I thought when I was your age—assuming that you are, what, 21, 23, 25 perhaps.

I was as infatuated with the specific nature of work, and took it for granted that *that* was the thing that defined you. Don't we all speak like that? 'I *am* a...'—not 'I am employed as a...' Coming out of college, I always defined the key thing as what I would do. Bureaucrat? MBA? Or, given my fascination with the uniform, the army? The police?

It was a given that *what* you did defined you more than anything else. Which is why those who got through IIT, IIM, AIIMS or the Civil Services sort of had their life made, since they would now be well paid or powerful professionals, and wasn't that what life was about?

It has taken me some time and some hard lessons to realise that I, like almost everyone else I knew, had got it wrong.

My learning here did not, unlike much else I have written about, come from practical experiences supported by some philosophy. This time, it came from thoughts and ideas that questioned my basics—from philosophy first. And then, as I took my time to understand and scrutinise what this philosophy was trying to tell me, and finally got—to a degree—the point, I began to look at the work I do from a rather different perspective. And as I did this learning, I had to do a lot of unlearning as well, since the very thought of 'I am a doctor/I am an army man/I am a journalist' is so deeply ingrained in our very sense of identity that it takes time to be seen with some detachment, from some distance.

The two—rather three—thoughts that came together to shape this slow but steady U-turn in my approach, and made me explore this idea further, have been—yes, again—tacked up around me; so I don't forget them, for many years now. You may have seen references to them earlier, in different contexts. I'll call them The Three for sake of simplicity through this chapter:

- We must act, but with equanimity, which is more important than any action. The question is not *what* shall we do, but *how* shall we do it? In what spirit shall we act?

  —S. Radhakrishnan, explaining II:53 from the Gita

- We find ourselves in the position for which we are fit, and if one has some capacity above another, the world will find that out too. He who grumbles at the little thing that has fallen to his lot, will grumble at everything. Always grumbling he will lead a miserable life. But that man who does his duty as he goes, putting his shoulder to the wheel, higher and higher duties will fall to his share...

  —Vivekananda

- There is no future in any job. The future lies in the man who does the job.

  —Anon

Over time, and over much thought, I began to realise that my initial glamourised thoughts about various kinds of jobs were, well, glamourised, and beyond that, essentially naive. All types of work appeal to the audience primarily because of what they bring out in us as individuals, don't they? We assume some traits to be a sort of given, at least when we haven't seen things from up close. Brave and fit soldiers; intelligent and philosophical professors; meticulous and creative architects; compassionate and sensitive doctors; well read and impartial journalists; etc., etc. We assume that most men with rifles posted on the nation's borders are patriotic. We have an impression that most models and actresses posing for cameras are dumb blondes. We are reasonably certain that most politicians have extremely low benchmarks of integrity.

While on a vague philosophical plane, I had already bought the idea behind The Three, what began to make more and more sense was the realisation over time that if *what* we did was the key, we would assume all doctors were compassionate, all soldiers were fiercely patriotic, all policemen honest and protective, all teachers intellectual and austere, all journalists well read and objective. But you can be a soldier and the *how* you do your job can still be shoddy, disinterested, lecherous and very 'unpatriotic'. You can be a doctor, and how you handle patients can still be mercenary, callous and utterly voyeuristic.

You can be a journalist, and how you handle your work can be egoistic, judgmental, totally subjective and manipulative. You can be a lawyer and have zilch respect for the law. Beyond a point, whether it's gloss and sheen you are looking at or whether you want to end your working day with the satisfaction of a good day's work done, what your visiting card says does *not* define you. We have all heard of the *love your job, don't love your company* line—I'd like to extend it to say, don't even love your job. It's a fickle affair. Love the *way* you do your job. Love your work style. Love your work fundamentals. Love your work philosophy. They are all that will stay with you, go with you from one place to another.

After all, your job is not *your* job in a real sense, more so if you are a paid employee. No matter what you think, you will never, ever have total control over what you do. In any case, this is not the economy that existed 30, 40 years back. Systems, structures, organisations, ways of doing things change constantly. Obsolescence strikes all around us all the time. What does *he/she is a very efficient telegraph operator* mean when there is no telegraph anymore? What does being an expert in two-stroke bike engines mean when emission laws mean such bikes are no longer being manufactured? What does specialisation in a software code mean when it's no longer in use? From IT to banking to journalism to whatever—a new way of doing things comes up every two or three years, and leaves you with no choice but to reinvent yourself professionally to even stay on the treadmill. The *what* you do isn't a static anymore—it can't be your USP. You have to make *how* you do things your USP.

You have to be your USP.

I retained a degree of sanity through my work years by replaying this thought on loop in my head over and over. I have often paid little attention to *what* my work on a given day was and obsessed endlessly over *how* I do it. I think it works. *What* you do may or may not have gold class written all over it; finally, the market, your company, your bosses, all take 70 per cent of the call on what you are assigned to do. Transfers, reallocations of work, of location, of priorities will always be out of your hands. So will the results. You could take the best calls as a publisher, a programmer, an engineer, and see the results blow up in your face. The best of movies have failed while the trashiest have raked in millions. Exceptional efforts in any number of work areas, when seen to fail with no logic as to why they did, are explained away with the *ahead of its time* argument. Being very, very good at what you do is no guarantee of success—sometimes it is the surest route to failure and to guaranteed peer hostility! Seeking satisfaction from the results of *what* you do, therefore, both in terms of the job you do and something specific you do in that job, is a gamble. I'd rather find that in *how* I do whatever work may come my way.

This may sound a little cynical—which it is not—but I sometimes find the *follow your dreams* and *when you really want something, the Universe will conspire to make it happen* lines a little like dollops of morphine, administered to make us believe that all will always be well. All we have to do is make up our minds. So endearing, but not so true. I mean, you may want to be a soldier, and join up, too—but if the economy is shrinking, there is total peace in the region and the government disbands your regiment altogether, how do you plan to stay a soldier? Create a private army? I may want to go to the moon—but ISRO needs to plan a manned mission to the moon before I can apply, I just can't fly that long on willpower alone. I can't control the 55 factors completely autonomous of me. All of you who know people who got laid off from their jobs when the economy got messy—well, how does your friend earn that promotion on account of his brilliance when his department is shut down altogether?

You can never, ever, be totally in command of exactly what you will end up doing, even though broadly you may be able to focus on the domains closer to your comfort levels—academic, sporting, cinema, soldiering, finance, whatever—and occasionally be lucky enough to find longevity in what interests you more. But you *can* take a 100 per cent call on how you do whatever your assignment may be. When the focus of your working shifts from what you do to how you do it, you become your own boss because you control 100 per cent of the most important part of your work while others obsess over what plum assignment they can gather next.

Reminder: What's all this getting at? It's getting at The Three. It's getting at reiterating—HOW you do the work you do is a far more important thing than WHAT you do.

When former Prime Minister V.P. Singh died, he got a one-column snippet on page 1 of the *Times of India*. When Sachin Tendulkar retired, he got the top half of most papers. This is not to say that the newspapers are the sole indexes of relevance; this is just to say even being a PM or a president—which I guess would come near the apex of what we can do—is not really as life changing as it may sound. Someone who plays cricket or chess or sings or plays the shehnai or makes rockets for space projects or whatever could be as relevant or powerful or popular based largely on the manner in which they are seen to do their tasks—essentially, the *how* they do becomes the key rather than what they do. A Lata Mangeshkar commands more clout, so to say, than many cabinet ministers—which is not because *what* she does—vocal music—is a more powerful occupational domain than politics, but because the *how* she does it puts her in a class of her own.

You see Gandhi every day. If nowhere else, on the currency notes in your purse. What did Gandhi do? He fought for freedom from a colonial regime. So did many, many others in that period of time in India and in many other colonised nations. What he was doing was creditable, but hardly unique. But Gandhi became a global figure and remains one to this day. His how—his obsession with non-violence and with a rulebook of peaceful agitation—differentiated him and effectively made him a case study, someone who commanded authority by virtue of who he was, not what position he held. Each time you take out a note to spend, remember that he's a global icon for how he fought for freedom, even in an era where fighting for freedom is increasingly done with an AK-47 slung across the fighter's shoulders.

In all areas—in almost all areas—if you can keep your first focus on how you work, it'll keep you stronger. Everyone thought Tihar Jail was a sidey posting till Kiran Bedi began to change how it was run and bagged a Magsaysay along the way. Fiat is a globally acknowledged leader in automobiles, owns some of the snazziest brands, but how unimpressively it's fared in India is a textbook story of the way it sells and services its cars in India has managed to mess it up to an almost irreversible state. On the contrary, the Mumbai dabbawallahs are not a global brand like Fiat—and what they do is very, very ordinary. They deliver lunchtime tiffins, period. And yet, they are not constrained by the ordinariness of the nature of their task. They relish what they do and work on how to do it better and better—and the how of their delivery system is what makes them a Six Sigma system and a globally recognised entity. It's a textbook case of making a mark not by what you do, but by how you do whatever you do.

This is not just about the modern economy, though—to reiterate, The Three are not really thoughts that have emerged in the last 10 years. Come to think of it, the Pandavas did a lot of things during exile and agyatvas which weren't in tune with their fundamental warrior reflex. Bhima was a cook, Arjuna a teacher of dance—and they did that reasonably well enough to not be found out, at least. They didn't just swing a mace or shoot off arrows throughout life. Excellence at work is an approach—to lock it just to the nature of work is myopic. It has to be linked to you—the doer of that work. Whatever work the combination of choice and chance brings your way, that must reflect how you do things. Then, you define work; the work you do on a given day doesn't define you. Instead of he/ she can do this job well, you want to hear, if you want a job done well, give it to him/her.

So let's not try to define ourselves by what we do. It's fickle. Instead, let's try to define ourselves by how we do what comes our way. It's far more coherent. And less depressing.

A thought to conclude: Have you noticed how obsessed we are with asking children, 'beta, bade ho kar aap kya banoge?' We think, as does the child, that the key thing is what he/she will do. Doctor banoonga, engineer banoonga, pilot banoonga, fauji banoonga, actor banoonga.

No child is ever asked, or ever explains, whether he/she will become an efficient or a callous teacher, a corrupt or a brave policeman, a mercenary or a compassionate doctor. That's apparently inconsequential.

Well, it isn't!

The Key Question is NOT what you will do. The Key Question is HOW you will do what you do. The what you do is about your interests, your inclinations. The how you do is about what you are, about what people will remember once you're dead and your brief stint as manager/commissioner/VP/editor/superstar/general busybody has come to an end.

And you need to get that clear, lest you spend most of your life living that delusion.

10

It's not about your *due*.
Systems outgrow you.
Accept, adapt

Much has been, and is, written about Maslow's need hierarchy, which places human needs in an ascending hierarchy, with the basic physiological needs—food, sleep, shelter—at the base and higher, more evolved self-actualisation needs, such as dignity, confidence and reputation at the apex.

In recent years, we have also read of the Hierarchy of Organisational Needs, which essentially puts the organisation in place of the individual and assesses what the organisation as a unit looks for, in what order of importance—for example, survival and stability at the bottom of the pyramid and reputation and CSR at the apex.

One of the key points of Maslow's thought is that a *fulfilled need is no longer a motivator*. From the side of those of us who work, it's like saying that a functional workstation, effective air conditioning and a proper washroom at the office are the base of the need hierarchy. If they aren't there, we'll be mightily irritated, but once they are, they aren't motivators. The same applies, in reverse, to how our workplace sees us, in some ways. There are things that, if not done, will irk the system, but if you think doing them will get you an upgrade or applause, you've got your basics very wrong and are headed for a very frustrating career.

What I see of the world around me suggests—to me at least—that the concept of the *Employer's Need Hierarchy vis-a-vis the Employee* is something all of us drawing salaries to work in workplaces need to understand. It'll spare us a lot of heartburn, angst and 'how can they?' analysis. I faced sporadic situations in my limited career at different points, especially when I was in my 20s, which made me pause and go into the 'how can they?' mode. I noticed identical sentiments in many similarly placed people in many other places.

Then, in the course of my extensive readings on random things, I read with bemusement how supercop K.P.S. Gill, at one point the de facto ruler of terrorism-infested Punjab in the late 1980s and early 1990s as the state's police chief, was summarily sent his retirement notice without the courtesy of prior intimation in a more peaceful Punjab which didn't depend on his counterterrorism skills anymore.

I read how the man who supposedly won the Battle of Britain for Britain, the chief of Fighter Command, Air Chief Marshal Dowding, was told to get lost not soon after the air threat from Germany was overcome, that too by means of a curt phone call telling him to vacate in 24 hours. The Air Council 'has no further work to offer you', read the note sent to him. Len Deighton writes in *Fighter*:

> As the air assault against England dwindled into harassing daylight attacks and a night offensive, the *RAF High Command acted more vindictively against the two men who had succeeded than did Göring (Luftwaffe Chief Hermann Göring) against the men who had failed.* Dowding and Park (Air Vice Marshal Keith R Park) had committed an unforgivable sin in the

eyes of the Air Ministry and their other critics: they had proved their theories right...That Dowding made so many enemies isn't surprising, but that the Air Ministry and the RAF should subject him to petty humiliations and harassments, even during the Battle, is one of the most extraordinary episodes of the war. That Churchill permitted it is a reflection upon that great man's judgment.[1] (Chaturvedi, emphasis added)

Deighton quotes Park as saying, many years later, 'To my dying day I shall feel bitter at the base intrigue which was used to remove Dowding and myself as soon as we had won the Battle of Britain.'

I don't want to feel bitter till my dying day about how anyone anywhere treated me professionally; so I spent more time reading this up.

I read about how the man who is often described as Germany's most outstanding soldier, Field Marshal Erwin Rommel, died not at the hands of the enemy but on the instructions of Adolf Hitler. The best summation of Rommel, and perhaps the greatest acknowledgment of his stature comes not from any German fan, but from Churchill. In *The Second World War: Vol. 3*, Churchill writes:

He (Rommel) was a splendid military gambler, dominating the problems of supply and scornful of opposition ... His ardor and daring inflicted grievous disasters upon us, but he deserves the salute which I made him—and not without some reproaches from the public—in the House of Commons in January 1942, when I said of him, We have a very daring and skillful opponent against us, and, may I say across the havoc of war, a great general.[2]

And how did the great general's career end? He did not fall to enemy fire or to assassination attempts. David Irving's *The Trail of The Fox* tells us that the 'great general' went up to his wife on 14 October 1944, and calmly said, 'In fifteen minutes I will be dead. On the Fuhrer's instructions I've been given a choice between taking poison or facing the People's Court. Stuplnages, Spiedel and Hofacker have implicated me in the 20 July conspiracy.'[3] It was indeed over in 15 minutes. He chose poison with his own hand, and died with his dignity intact.

While the details of what led Hitler to believe charges levelled against Rommel, by officers implicated in an anti-Hitler plot, are too long to be explained here, Irving sums up the sentiment succinctly:

> How ironic that he, Erwin Rommel, who has survived
> enemy killer squads, bombs, aircraft cannon-fire, tank
> shells and rifle bullets in two world wars, should have
> to die now because of a failed conspiracy to which he
> has never been a party, organised by a General Staff to
> which he did not belong!

I found the odd similarity on both warring sides with supposedly divergent philosophies even more fascinating: British Air Marshal does a very difficult job, negates the efforts of Hitler's friend and Luftwaffe's boss Göring, effectively saves Britain from invasion—and is trashed by Churchill. German Field Marshal does an outstanding job for much of his career—is praised by Churchill—and is effectively sentenced to death by Hitler.

And you think *you* have boss problems?

I read about how US General Douglas MacArthur, the man who ruled post-war occupied Japan, and who later coined the phrase 'old soldiers never die, they just fade away', ended his career by being summarily dismissed by President Truman while he was the commander of US forces in the Korean War for making public statements that contradicted Truman's policies. I read about General Patton, a man with a very aggressive military reputation, who may well have ended his career the same way if he hadn't died in a road mishap shortly after the war was over—his belligerence and outspokenness often overshadowed his military skills.

I read about innumerable instances of officers, Generals, employees who seemingly did a great job and yet were lost to anonymity or discarded—sometimes temporarily, sometimes permanently—by the systems which once feted them. I read—with a sense of delicious irony—about Churchill, who was instrumental in Dowding's exit, losing the general elections in Britain immediately after he had won the war. I read about innumerable civil servants in the Indian bureaucracy who were sent to complex, risky or challenging assignments to 'clean up the mess' and who cleaned it up, and were soon after tossed aside and made to look and feel very dispensable indeed. The uniformed services, in particular, often have a sense of grievance about police or paramilitary officers being sent to the forefront of anti-terror operations when the going gets really tough, and later—once the going is not so tough because they did what they were told to—they spend the rest of their lives defending themselves legally. Think Punjab and the anti-terror heroes of the Congress regimes being locked up for human rights violations when the Akalis came to power, for instance.

I evolved my own personal theories about how governments in India needed the more neutral, strong-willed, efficient administrators to run areas that were terrorism hubs or riot prone or otherwise falling apart; but once those areas were under control, they preferred to place officers who were more flexible, not too rule-centric and usually friendlier to the ruling party. I saw how a Vajpayee ended up, in my view, drifting out of relevance for the BJP in a way similar to how Gandhi drifted out of immediate relevance for the Congress; the parties rode on the appeal and charisma of the leader, but did not want to be tied down to the specifics of the thought and ideology beyond a point. I saw how L.K. Advani was relevant for the BJP when it jumped from two Lok Sabha seats to 119, but was no longer relevant when it wanted to move from the 100-somethings to 272 and beyond. I saw that it was perhaps even in organisational interest to be this way—the Congress refused to move beyond the family surname and lived in nostalgia and past glory, and see where that landed it.

I came to the conclusion that *there is no such thing as a universally accepted definition of 'good work.'* What is perceived to be *good work* constantly changes with time and context. Those of us who think that we will do what *we* see as *good work* and, therefore, will be automatically rewarded with more money and more appreciation and bigger cabins on a recurring basis on that account are placed somewhere between naive and dumb.

The point is, our organisations expect us to do things, in an ascending hierarchy. At each point, of course, if we *don't* do what is expected, we'll run into trouble. But once you've done something—delivered that project, built that building, got that market share, launched that product, won that war—that fulfilled need *is no longer a motivator* for your employer.

Look at it this way. What is the first, most basic work output? Turning up to work. If you don't punch your card or reach an hour late, it'll become a bone of contention between you and your system, perhaps HR or more likely your immediate boss. The company's primary need from you, at the bottom of its need pyramid, is simply your presence. Not turning up for work is the simplest and surest way to get shot, right?

Once you are there, though, you can't really expect a thank-you note from HR for having punched in your card. That was a very basic need. It's fulfilled. It's no longer a motivator for anything; it's not in the mental frame of anyone. You won't get a higher increment for 80 per cent attendance. Now, you'll discuss work quantity. If that's not adequate, you'll have meetings. Once you meet work quantity benchmarks, they will not be talked about. The need will be for greater quality in the delivery of that quantity. When you meet all of that, if all your KRAs are in place, the expectation will shift to KBAs, especially if you have to handle the smallest of coordination/communication/supervisory roles. When you're done with X, X is not a motivator. So nostalgia, reflection and gloating over past success are not the fundamental traits of systems that employ you—and they never will be, no matter where you work or what you do. I will not spend money on any of Ram Gopal Verma's recent films—no offence, Ramu—just because he made *Rangeela* or *Sarkaar* once upon a time.

Past output is irrelevant. The same applies to us. There are no carry-forwards in careers. Think of it as CL, and each day as December 31st—either you've managed it or it's lapsed.

Don't think you can ask for more CL next year because you worked 365 days this one. Doesn't work that way, and understanding that will lessen the heartburn.

As we go around earning our daily bread in whatever field of work we are engaged in, a few of us will be lucky enough to have uninterrupted tenures and more than our due share of credit. Most, however, will not. That builds angst, nostalgia, bitterness and sometimes a sense of betrayal, of having been dealt an unfair deal. It's completely natural. It's also totally useless. The notion that we have earned a lifelong pass that entitles us to be treated with veneration and respect because of the great work we did in the past is an overly romanticised and completely unrealistic one—and it usually leads to drinks and grouses being nursed long after they ought to.

Lalit Modi may have for all practical purposes created the IPL—that didn't help when the parent body of the IPL got together to chuck him out. Do you recall the margin when the BCCI voted to expel him? 29-0. 29-Z-E-R-O. If the BCCI on a given day can so summarily discard Modi, and if Apple can ask Steve Jobs to move on, if Ekta Kapoor can replace her best-selling TV actors—actors who perhaps thought they made the serials work—with a snap of her fingers when she feels like with no loss of TRPs, I'm not sure if any of us have the legitimate right to look up and groan, 'Why *me*, God? After *everything* that I've done, do I *still* need to prove myself?' Er, yes. God may well smirk and say, 'Look around—whoever gave you the idea it was only you, eh?'

Sometimes what we don't do makes a bigger statement than what we do. I was thoroughly engaged by the story of coach Kabir Khan in *Chak De! India*, and by the manner in which he held his disparate team of skilled, yet complex, individuals together till they won global acclaim. But more than that, for me, *the* defining moment of what the character was about came when the victorious team landed back home to applause and flashbulbs—and Kabir Khan was conspicuous by his absence. Having been maligned earlier, it was essentially a personal battle that Kabir had fought, and having proven what he had to, he could just get up and walk away. He didn't need credit—and so he couldn't have been hurt at being denied it either, or cringe if he was slighted, ignored, forgotten or replaced.

By keeping away from the post-victory moment of glory, and instead heading to what really mattered to him, by having little interest in waving his hands and soaking in the applause and strutting around, saying 'I told you so', he demonstrated what is so often lost in the endless cycle of proving yourself at whatever you do—class.

The moral of this story: Once you have fulfilled the need for which you were hired, you always, always have to cater to a higher need or risk being irrelevant. Unless your dad or mom runs your company. Actually, even if they *do* run your company—just ask Rahul Gandhi.

Notes

1. Deighton, Len. (1979). *The True Story of the Battle of Britain: Fighter*. St Albans, Herts: Triad/ Panther Books.
2. Churchill, Winston. (2005). *The Grand Alliance: The Second World War* (Vol. 3). London: The Penguin Group.
3. Irving, David. (1977). *The Trail of the Fox*. Great Britain: Weidnefeld and Nicolson.

Postscript

All the random philosophy that has come your way in these pages is not borne out of academic research. Or out of the attempt to present some fine academic self-help manual, some Chicken Soup for The Struggling Professional or a How to Win over Colleagues and Influence Bosses sort of manual.

It's come from earning a modest salary, starting at some ₹4,300 a month in the backwaters of a nondescript location in a small town, and not having an MBA or something like that to tell me how to structure or plan a career. It has come from making many, many mistakes. It has also come from seeing so many things happen around me, so many live lessons broadcast in our face, which we simply have to pick and use, gratis, and which teach us more than a fancy lecture by a life *guru* ever could.

I was still in school when I saw Gavaskar's batting in a phase where Indian batsmen could do little against the fearsome West Indian pace attack of Marshall, Holding, Garner, etc., and it was not so much the runs he made as the way he approached the task which made me pay attention when he spoke of the mindset behind it—of staying at the crease in difficult times, of not selling your wicket cheap, of not playing to the gallery and throwing it away. I saw pretty much every ball of two of the greatest innings I remember watching—Gavaskar's 96 in his final Test and V.V.S. Laxman's 281 in *the* Test against Australia—and subconsciously absorbing more from them than I ever could have from pages of pure philosophy. In a really, really bad situation, you can't swagger around. Put your head down. Play one ball at a time. Don't get frustrated. Don't let them choke you. Don't lose the mind game being played. Stay at the crease. Stay at the crease. Stay at the crease!

I saw how Vinod Kambli's and Sachin Tendulkar's careers went very, very different ways after running parallel right from school to the initial entry into team India. I saw that a man may be born with as much skill as a compatriot—may be more—but if he does not keep his head on his shoulders, does not know how to not get intoxicated and lose focus in the heady moments, he is at best a sprinter, he can't run a marathon and will often have to look to the past to see his highest phase in life. Years later, when Shoaib Akhtar, clearly the fastest bowler Pakistan had at that point, was someone whom no captain wanted in his team because of his temperament; I explained his situation often to a flamboyant photographer or a reporter in my team who was individually quite good at what he or she did, but a disaster when it came to working in a team and explained that finally, when your weakness in team skills becomes greater than your strength in work skills, you could perhaps be a standalone genius, but nobody running a team will have the energy to humour you all the time, and finally you'll be dropped.

I saw how Saurav Ganguly and Greg Chappell's clash finally ended up damaging the both of them, and realised that letting personal animosity get the better of you is finally something that trivialises you in some way, no matter who wins. Even the winner loses in such spats. I also admired Ganguly's guts and ability to come back into the team—this time not as a skipper—and how he became the Man of The Series in his comeback effort. That, to my mind, was a man playing for his reputation, not for endorsements or stats. Ganguly's quasi-arrogant refusal to roll over and die no matter how many things were lined up against him at least made him an intriguing figure to watch, no matter whether you agreed with his calls or not.

I read about how Ronald Reagan, Hollywood-star-turned-American-Prez, towards the end of his days, did not even recall that he was the president of the USA, and that almost frightened me. To not even have a sense of satisfaction at having done something of consequence made the illusions of power look so trivial, and the lobbying and stress for the utterly trivial power that office politics entails seem so pathetically inconsequential. I saw how former Prime Ministers Gujral and Deve Gowda were hardly noticed wherever they went. I saw how V.P. Singh—the messiah of Mandal, the architect who reshaped India's social structure, etc., etc.—died with the country and the media barely batting an eyelid, with nobody giving a damn. I saw how Narasimha Rao faded away once no longer in power, how Atal Behari Vajpayee seemed to have been tucked away out of sight and out of mind as a physically incapacitated man of little consequence as the next generation of his party, younger and more virile, took centrestage. And I looked around and asked—if even being the

prime minister is so transitional and is no pro-
tector against loneliness, sidelining and sliding
into oblivion as you wait for your time to run
out, what's the big deal, the arrogance of power?
What will a salaried job give you, for which you
have to lose your mind? Work; don't go mad in
the race. What life has to bring your way, it will.
Don't lose it over denied promotions and *power*
taken away—there never was any, to begin
with. And it is here that I began to understand
that Krishna wasn't cracking a practical joke at
Arjuna's expense when he spoke about working
for the sake of work, not the rewards. He was
actually talking sense.

I often saw people crib about someone else
getting ahead because of connections, influence, clout, looks, sex appeal, money, whatever.
I am not saying it doesn't happen. Of course it
happens. But my point to the cynics around me
was—OK, so X's dad has clout in the BCCI. So,
X gets inexplicably picked for team India ahead
of better contenders. Right. His dad will get him
in the team—but how will his dad manage the
curator of the pitch in Sydney to get a slow track
made, or ask the Aussie bowlers not to pitch
the ball short to Munna dearest? How much can
be *managed*, beyond a time? If Munna's middle

stump goes flying three times in four matches, or he closes his eyes each time Brett Lee unleashes a bouncer aimed at his nose, even Daddy can't do much beyond a point.

Once, in a team meeting, a colleague asked me, 'But why are you going to interview Katrina? Whatever she has done is because she is Salman's girlfriend!' My limited counter argument was that we are being silly if we attribute everything to that because, by that logic, every actress who at some point has been Salman's girlfriend (and that is some list) should have done exactly as much as Katrina has. Which they haven't. 'Salman can perhaps get her a role. But even he can't make people come and watch the movie,' was my point, and by extension I have learnt not to overrate what any sort of connection or link can do for a career. You have to know what you do, and do it well, else nothing works. Hrithik's dad launched him, yes—but people liked the film! That is what made him a star—not daddy. If dad making you the hero in your debut film was all that was required, we wouldn't have half a dozen kids in Bollywood being launched and re-launched and frustratingly re-re-launched, like how ISRO's launch missions used to be in the years when I was in school. They kept crashing into the sea shortly after take-off and then the whole thing happened all over again after six months. Dad can make you a lead actor in his production, period. He can't make you a star—and he can't go out and make everyone buy tickets to watch your dead-pan face. And SRK's dad didn't produce a film to launch him. For that matter, Sachin's dad wasn't a big shot in the BCCI, and Narendra Modi or Arvind Kejriwal's dads weren't chief ministers anywhere. So what's to envy about having Big Daddies to launch you anywhere? On the contrary, for most of their lives, they live in the shadow of being where they are, having got that role or that seat because of their surname. Not good for the ego, no, not good at all to be called baba at 40. I wouldn't want that.

Talking of SRK, you would learn as much about surviving and growing at the workplace from watching Chak De! as you would by reading half dozen assorted managerial handbooks. I, in particular, found it a reference point for so many things, perhaps also because when it released, I was professionally in the position of being, in effect, the coach of a good but volatile team of sometimes—OK, frequently!—warring girls. I had my reference points in my head for most of the episodes—the instigation of the vacillating group against Kabir Khan by a disgruntled lot, the pressure on those inclined towards his methods by those who hated him, the insinuations of the captain being made captain not because she was good but because he had a 'soft corner' for her, the frustration at the refusal of the best players to play as a team and to pass the ball to each other, preferring individual glory, even the 'Bindiya Naik' moments—those of you who have watched the movie would remember the scene where she partially unzips her track jacket and asks him, in context of the skipper, 'What does she have that I don't?'

I learnt a lot from that movie—I practically absorbed it—and it gave me reference points for many things which I then imbibed, most of which are scattered across the earlier pages of this book. Among the foremost was the ability of Kabir Khan to come back and coach, without rancour, the same girls who had signed off on the petition asking him to be removed as their coach, without holding it against them. That is not an easy thing to do. When sometimes my best reporters got involved in ego clashes over bylines, I sat them down and ran them through the star scorers versus Kabir Khan tussle, reminding them that they were simply playing out a template, where individual glory and credit was coming ahead of the need to beat the competition, much to the coach's annoyance. And I learnt one thing that I was not very good at—working with, giving a fair chance to even those whom you may personally find dealing with very unwelcome. For years now, when I have hired, promoted or given a key task to someone whom I clearly have a lack of personal equation with, perhaps even outright hostility, and someone has come up to me with an inquisitive look at the unexpected decision, my unapologetically filmy answer has been, 'I don't care if Bindiya Naik detests Kabir Khan, and vice versa; if Bindiya Naik is the one who can score in this match, Bindiya Naik will play!' If I ever do something in life of consequence, I will have to give credit to Jaideep Sahni, Chak De!'s scriptwriter.

And there was another thing I loved about the attitude that Kabir Khan had. Lots of people are sorted under pressure, but just lose it when handling success. I once wrote a piece for the TOI's Speaking Tree on it—and it is with that, that I will conclude this chapter and this book. I hope it makes some sense to you. For me, these aren't points about handling office—they're fundamentally about how we live and what we leave behind when we move on. There is little point in being powerful at work and having no one come to your funeral. I've seen that happen, more than once. I'd like to be powerful, and do something of consequence, but I'd also like to have a few people take a half day off from work when I'm dead, out of just giving the Devil his due, if not out of affection.

Wouldn't you?

Why Kabir Khan's absence at the moment of triumph marks his presence the most[1]

Towards the end of the story in the Bollywood film *Chak De! India* when the hockey team returns triumphant, ready to relish all the attention, coach Kabir Khan is conspicuous by his absence. He prefers instead to go reclaim a home he had left in disgrace many years earlier. Why does Kabir not wish to bask in his moment of glory, after erasing the stigma that he carried for years?

It took him seven years—after a failure saw him shunned, ostracised and branded as a traitor—to gather the strength to redeem himself. Taking up an unlikely challenge, he met with cynicism and indifference. He met further resistance from the very individuals he tried to shape into a team.

His past record, integrity and judgement were all questioned. Even the players who seemingly believed in him succumbed to peer pressure; he saw the team apparently united for only one goal, that of ousting him. Confronted with this, yet refusing to do things differently, he all but walked out. The innuendo and slander continued even after that storm blew over. At many points, the opposing teams were the least of his challenges.

All through this, Kabir did not question his fundamentals or his approach; neither did he become vicious in his responses. Whether officials or players applauded or smirked, he stood his ground. He was no longer concerned about disdain, once he believed in what he was doing. And he was equally unconcerned about gathering adulation after having proved himself.

He had, simply put, outgrown the need for both. Rudyard Kipling wrote of treating triumph and disaster just the same, but that is easier said than done. The moments that test our reactions are when the anchors that hold our sense of self-worth are forced loose. These are moments when we can only look within to know that we are right, while few seem to agree and most are indifferent. Those moments tell us whether our consciousness has grown in strength, or whether the absence of support breaks us.

Explaining verse 38 in the Gita's second chapter, S. Radhakrishnan describes the man who has discovered his true end of life:

> Though everything else is taken away from him, though he has to walk the streets, cold, hungry and alone, though he may know no human being into whose eyes he can look and find understanding, he shall yet be able to go his way with a smile on his lips, for he has gained inward freedom.

The strength to know no one in whose eyes he could find understanding, and yet go his way without wavering, is the strength that Kabir Khan displayed. It is the strength we need if we are to live without being at the mercy of world opinion. That strength comes from within, from understanding our real nature.

Rejection and failure can spur us to know ourselves, to go beyond the world's parameters of praise and criticism. Kabir was unfairly made to bear a cross for seven years. It could happen to any one of us. One of the most unfair verdicts ever was given to the man who was literally nailed to a cross. But He faced crucifixion with courage, and He was the one who had the strength to get resurrected. If we know and believe in ourselves even when the rest find it convenient to crucify us, we would have the strength to resurrect ourselves too.

Note

1. First published in *The Times of India*. 2007. 'The Speaking Tree', 6 September.

About the Author

Anshul Chaturvedi began his journalism career as a hard news journalist, in 1996, and shortly thereafter became the editor of local English dailies based in Jammu, specialising in topics such as the Kashmir militancy and the ISI, an unlikely starting point for someone currently managing lifestyle content in Delhi. He then moved out of J&K to work with *The Times of India*'s (*TOI*'s) launch edition, in Chandigarh, in the year 2000. He was temporarily sent on deputation to the features section, but it soon became his primary work area, which it has been since then. He was then posted to Lucknow and worked as editor of multiple products across Uttar Pradesh (U.P.) for four years, attempting to bring Karva Chauth parties on page 3, while writing on U.P. politics for the *TOI*'s edit page. In 2005, he was brought to the capital, and so began his journalistic stint in Delhi as the editor of the

Delhi Times. In the past few years, that role has expanded to include charge of many similar supplements in North India, and today he oversees features teams in about a dozen cities.

While he attempts to scrutinise high society and the glam world from the vantage point of his primary job as the *Delhi Times'* editor, personally, he spends time reading through the likes of Vivekananda, Iacocca and Covey, watching cricket and consuming everything on the Second World War and Subhash Bose that he can find. A collection of his interviews with the three Khans of Bollywood over the past decade was published in the form of a book, *Uncut* (2013). He is also an occasional writer on his version of everyday philosophy for *The Speaking Tree*.